SHADOWS OF DEATH

SHADOWS OF DEATH

By the Editors of Time-Life Books

TIME-LIFE BOOKS, ALEXANDRIA, VIRGINIA

CONTENTS

POMP AND CIRCUMSTANCE

As the writer William Saroyan neared the conclusion of a long and full life, he feigned surprise at his approaching death, claiming that he had thought an exception would be made in his case.

Wit is not the usual response to the prospect of death, but no event inspires a fuller range of emotions. Grief alone takes countless forms, from private tears and simple words to enormous social convulsions and treasury-draining acts of homage. Many cultures, viewing the dead with fear, have devised rites to hasten them on their way and keep them in their place.

Other societies have focused on loving remembrance and even active support for those who, presumably, have gone on to the afterlife. And some of the most powerful reactions of all have been those that anticipate death—the years spent preparing for it, the deep-seated ambivalence toward it, the funeral arrangements that allow for the possibility of revival.

A King for All Time

Charlemagne, king of the Franks from AD 768 to 814, was a towering figure in a turbulent age. As though bent on reconstituting the shattered glories of Rome, he conquered fractious tribes all across Western Europe, welded them into a great Christian empire, promoted literacy and learning, promulgated laws, and ruled with an iron hand until pleurisy felled him at the age of seventy-two.

According to one glorious account of Charlemagne's burial rites, the officers of the court made sure that their sovereign would be a king for all eternity. They embalmed his body, dressed him in his royal mantle, strapped on his sword, put a chalice in his hand, placed the Gospels on his lap and his scepter and gold shield at his feet, and sat him on a gold throne in a sepulchral vault in the basilica of Aix-la-Chapelle, the German city that Charlemagne had created.

The account is probably mostly myth—myth inspired by the almost religious reverence Charlemagne inspired, and myth that grew and was embellished over time. In his own day, many people refused to accept that he was dead: They said—as it would be said of the legendary King Arthur—that he was merely sleeping and would awake to rescue them at a time of crisis. Some believed that his beard would continue to grow until it had circled the tomb three times, at which point the world would come to an end.

Although the reality of Charlemagne's burial was not quite up to the myth, it was nevertheless still fit for a king. On the day of his death, his body was carefully washed and dressed in royal garments, and a chain with a golden cross was placed around his neck. It was probably dusk when he was laid to rest in the basilica at Aix-la-Chapelle in an ancient white marble sarcophagus ornamented with bas-relief carving.

In 1165, the Holy Roman Emperor Frederick Barbarossa, who counted Charlemagne as his illustrious predecessor, had the Frankish king's bones transferred from the marble sarcophagus to an even more elaborate golden shrine. □

For more than 800 years, the remains of the Christian emperor Charlemagne (above) have rested in this elaborately sculpted golden shrine in the basilica at Aix-la-Chapelle.

Fatherly Farewell

Willie "the Wimp" Stokes cut quite a figure on Chicago's South Side. Involved in gambling and other doubtful activities, he was a sharp dresser and an owner of late-model Cadillacs—until he was gunned down by unknown assailants outside a motel in 1984 at the age of twenty-eight.

The funeral arrangements were made by his father, Willie "Flukey" Stokes, a well-known drug dealer who himself would be shot to death three years later. Flukey opted for a top-of-the-line burial that would suit his late son's tastes in travel. "One year I was in debt and he sold his Cadillac to help me out," ex-plained Flukey Stokes to an interviewer from *Jet* magazine. "So I owed him one." More than 2,000 people came to a South Side funeral home to see the results, which did not disappoint: There was Willie the Wimp *(above)*, wearing a flaming red suit and wide-brimmed gray hat, propped up in a steel coffin that had been endowed with an authentic Cadillac grill, a plastic windshield, styrofoam tires and steering wheel, flashing headlights and taillights, and miniature license plates bearing the letters *W-I-M-P.* A massive diamond gleamed on the ring finger of the departed's left hand, and he clutched five $100 bills. "I think he would have really liked it because that's the way he was," said his mother. "He was flashy and he believed in style."

The coffin had cost some $7,000, but Flukey Stokes saved on expenses by removing the $100 bills and the diamond before his son was put into the ground. □

Fashions come and go in burial clothing. For guidance in its designs, Rita Barber Creations of Abilene, Texas—America's largest supplier of burial garments—watches the trendsetting attire of such television news personalities as Sam Donaldson and David Brinkley.

A Stopped Clock

Hannah Beswick, a well-to-do eighteenth-century resident of Manchester, England, regarded dying as fraught with uncertainty. According to some explanations of her outlook, her own brother had been declared dead while frozen in a catatonic trance and had escaped burial only by stirring in his coffin at the last moment. How could she be sure that she would not be buried alive because of some similar mistake? The answer, Beswick decided, was to avoid being buried at all.

Although the details of Hannah Beswick's story are murky, it appears that she secretly instructed her physician, Dr. Charles White, to embalm her when she appeared to die; he was then to keep her above ground and make regular inspections of the corpse to detect any signs of revival.

After she passed away in 1758 at the age of seventy, White followed these instructions to the letter, his sense of duty no doubt buttressed by the sizable sum of £400 her will allocated to funeral expenses. Pondering the question of where to keep her, he settled on a container much less obtrusive than a coffin: He placed her upright in the case of a grandfather clock. For easy scrutiny, her head was positioned where the clock face would ordinarily have been; a veil spared bypassers the startling sight of a corpse.

In the years that followed, White kept the clock-coffin in a small museum of curious medical and scientific items he had amassed, faithfully monitoring its inmate to make sure her condition was final. After Dr. White's own death in 1813, the container was turned over to another doctor, who subsequently left it to the Manchester Natural History Society. It remained there until 1868, when museum officials concluded that it was "an undesirable relic." Noting for the record that Miss Hannah Beswick had been convincingly dead for more than a hundred years, they had the body interred in a local cemetery. □

Underground Art

Carpenter Kane Kwei was attending the funeral of a fellow Ga tribesman in Ghana when he was struck by an inspiration he calls divine: The ceremony would be more festive if, instead of the traditional wrapping of mats or cloth, the body was buried in an elaborately carved coffin whose shape represented some aspect of the individual's life.

Kwei's custom coffins caught on among the Ga, and the carpenter found himself running a large workshop with apprentices. He turned out such carved creations as fish, whales, boats and outboard motors for fishermen, cocoa pods for farmers, airplanes for frequent travelers, and a hen with chicks clustered around her feet for a woman with a large brood of children.

Increasingly, affluent Ghanaians shun the old-style wrappings for a more artistic and individualistic way of honoring their dead. Other carpenters, some former apprentices to Kwei, have set up on their own, making coffins that sell for as much as $1,600. Nor is all of the handiwork of Kwei and his followers destined to go into the ground. Their made-to-order coffins are now prized objects in the collections of art connoisseurs worldwide. □

Artist Paa Joe, who learned his craft from pioneer coffin carver Kane Kwei, fashioned this casket for a Ghanaian onion farmer.

The Road to Beyond

Sandra Ilene West lived life in the fast lane, and she had no intention of changing her style when she died. A one-time Hollywood model, she married Ike West, heir to a Texas oil-and-cattle fortune, in 1965. Three years later, he died of a drug overdose in Las Vegas, and in 1977, at the age of thirty-six, his widow met the same fate. But she had scripted a characteristically flamboyant last act: Perhaps mindful of ancient kings who were buried with their chariots, she composed a will bequeathing her millions to

Ike West's brother (whom she had once dated) on the condition that she be buried beside her husband "in my Ferrari, with the seat slanted comfortably." Sandra West also stipulated that she be dressed in her lace nightgown.

The will was protested by her lawyer, who produced a second document purportedly leaving most of her fortune to him. A court disagreed, ruling that her "unusual, but not illegal" burial scheme could go forward. Shortly thereafter, an enormous crate holding a baby-blue

Ferrari with the nightgowned West at the wheel was lowered into an enormous grave in a San Antonio cemetery. To prevent vandals from getting at the sporty vehicle, the crate was surrounded with steel mesh and covered with concrete. □

Superimposed over a photograph of her crated remains and car being lowered into the grave, Ferrari fanatic Sandra West poses on the hood of her sports coupe.

Call from the Grave

The age-old dread of premature burial was still commonplace early in this century, and with reason. Physicians of solid repute cited numerous instances of people being pronounced dead and then stirring to life again, reviving from a coma or some trauma that had reduced the pulse or respiration to imperceptibility. To guard against such horrific errors, ancient Romans had kept bodies under close watch for days before sealing them away from the world. To make doubly sure, the Romans cut a finger off the corpse before cremation to see whether fresh blood flowed from the wound. Some later societies tested corpses for lingering vitality by applying a hot iron or boiling water.

In the eighteenth and nineteenth centuries, scientific-minded inventors devised a range of new gadgets employing bells and buzzers to allow anyone buried prematurely to send distress signals from the grave. These mechanical wizards also designed breathing devices to keep victims alive until they could summon help and be dug up.

One well-received contraption was designed in the late nineteenth century by Russian nobleman Count Karnicé-Karnicke. He reportedly addressed himself to the task after attending the funeral of a young girl; as earth was shoveled onto her coffin, she awakened from her deathly state and began to scream piteously—a moment that haunted him forever after. The count's dual-function apparatus provided for both breathing and signaling. Before the coffin was covered with earth, a long tube was inserted through a small hole in its top at a point above the inmate's chest. The tube extended above ground level to a lidded metal box, which normally remained closed to prevent the escape of noxious gases as flesh decayed. From the lid of the box, a spring ran down through the tube to a glass ball suspended over the body; at the slightest breath, the ball would release the spring, causing the box to fly open and allowing the entry of air. At the same time, a flag would pop up from the box, a light would flash, and a bell with enough power to ring for thirty minutes would sound the alarm. The not-dead-after-all inhabitant of the coffin could also speak through the tube (designed to enhance even the feeblest whisper).

The need for measures such as Karnicé-Karnicke's against mistaken burial began to dissipate as medical science developed more reliable methods for measuring the body's functions. A flat line on an electroencephalogram usually leaves little room for dreadful doubt: Death is the diagnosis. □

Although an awakening victim of premature burial could manually trigger this lifesaving device, a single breath was enough to displace the glass globe in the casket, raising a flag, admitting air, and ringing an alarm bell.

Eternal Ease

Reuben John Smith struck his neighbors in Amesbury, Massachusetts, as an unassuming sort of fellow. He arrived in town from Buffalo after the Civil War, worked as a hack driver, and enjoyed playing checkers in his free time. At some point, well before his death at the age of seventy-one in 1899, Smith began mulling over his own funeral arrangements. Some people speculated that he must have been afraid of underground burial, while others said he was merely being sensible: Smith apparently had no family, and if he did not make funeral plans for himself he would have to take potluck when the time came.

Whatever the reason, Smith came up with a satisfying scheme. Using a good portion of his small income to pay for it, he had a sturdy tomb built of brick and white Vermont marble and fitted with a heavy steel door. While this structure stood ready at the local cemetery, Smith chose and purchased a fine oak chair upholstered in russet leather. He wished, he explained, to be buried "in a sitting position in a reclining chair." These preparations completed, he reportedly visited the tomb frequently in order to savor the view. Sometimes he invited a guest to join him.

Smith died in his cramped apartment, and his funeral was held there. In accordance with his wishes, he was strapped to the leather chair, draped with a black shroud, and conveyed by wagon to his tomb. He was arranged facing the door, and the shroud was removed so that mourners filing past could have a last look at their comfortably seated friend. □

No Place Like Home

In the sixty-foot-long grand hall of Harriet Douglas's upstate New York castle was solid evidence of the heiress's imperious, often eccentric ways. After an acrimonious divorce in 1850 ended her late, brief marriage to a tedious lawyer named Cruger, Douglas had the marriage bed sawed in half. The two objects thus produced were hauled downstairs to serve simultaneously as couches and as expressions of her marital sentiments.

Douglas loved her great stone pile of a place, which she had been inspired to build on her Mohawk Valley estate in 1832 after visiting the castle of cousins in Scotland. (An inveterate globetrotter in her youth, she boldly collected prominent personages and became friends with the likes of Sir Walter Scott and William Wordsworth.) She maintained a house in New York City as well, where she was a pillar of blue-blooded society. But her heart was at Henderson House, so named for the original owner of the land that it stood on.

At some point in time, an inspiration struck the grande dame: Her heart—and indeed, the rest of her too—could remain at Henderson House forever. She determined that the castle's cellar would be her burial place, and she ordered granite from Scotland for a grandiose sarcophagus. It was duly carved and installed in readiness for Douglas's demise, and her instructions were spelled out in her will.

But she was foiled by her heirs. When the eighty-two-year-old Douglas died in 1872, her family broke her will and gave her a thoroughly conventional burial in a New York City churchyard. But what to do with the sarcophagus? Some practical soul had it hauled out of the cellar and installed outside, where it became a water trough for horses. Eventually the sarcophagus disintegrated. Some say years of freezing split the granite into pieces, while others ascribe its destruction to a bolt of lightning. Harriet Douglas would have undoubtedly preferred the latter explanation. □

Harriet Douglas *(inset)* wished to be buried in the basement of Henderson House *(below)*, her imposing estate in New York, but was thwarted by her heirs.

Practice Makes Perfect

Jim Gernhart was a practical man. On the plains of western Kansas, he ran a general store and operated a farm, achieving considerable prosperity before retiring and moving to Burlington, Colorado, in the mid-1940s to live with his sister. His sister died a few years later, and he was not happy with her funeral, which seemed to him somehow abrupt and impersonal. So he began to ponder his own passing. The possibility that he might receive a similarly inadequate funeral so dismayed Gernhart that, in 1951, still spry at seventy-five, he decided to make a test run.

At first, the townsfolk did not like the notion of rehearsing a funeral. A preacher Gernhart hired for the occasion backed out, and the hymn singers followed suit. But when Gernhart showed no signs of giving up on the idea—and when brief but worldwide attention was focused on him—Burlington changed its collective mind. The practice corpse became a source of local pride.

The last-rites run-through came off splendidly. Eight Burlington businessmen served as pallbearers, carrying the handsome casket Gernhart had purchased—a solid copper model with a peach-colored satin and velour lining. Upwards of half of the small town's 2,200 inhabitants attended the service in the local armory. ("Does a man good to see so many people out to bury him," said a gratified Gernhart.) The preacher was lavish in his praise of the hypothetically departed, describing him as an unselfish man who had done a number of kindnesses for other people. Jim Gernhart's eyes grew moist as he listened and watched. "Real nice funeral, ain't it?" he was overheard to remark.

The cost of the test run was estimated at $4,000, but Gernhart considered himself amply paid back in reassurance. And the reward continued. For several years thereafter, Gernhart and his ever-ready casket remained the main attractions in any parade the town held. But it was not until 1980, when Jim Gernhart died in a rest home at the age of 103, that Burlington's nearly three decades of practice were finally put to use. □

In nearly three decades of rehearsing for his 1980 funeral, Jim Gernhart wore out the lining of the solid copper casket that he bought himself in 1951, when he was seventy-five.

A Storm of Woe and Wrath

One of the wildest outpourings of grief in modern times was unleashed by the death—from a heart attack after surgery—of the eighty-nine-year-old Ayatollah Ruhollah Khomeini in 1989. An implacable Muslim fundamentalist who detested both Westerners and moderates in his own Islamic world, he had led a revolution in Iran that overthrew the shah in 1979. For the next ten years, he ruled as the supreme authority in religious and political spheres, which he saw as inextricably linked. To many of his countrymen, his passing was a cataclysm.

On June 5, Khomeini lay in state in a refrigerated glass coffin on a funeral bier atop a dusty hill in Teheran, and hundreds of thousands of Iranians massed for a final glimpse of him. Eight people were crushed to death, and hundreds of others were injured in the press of the crowd. The next day, more than a million mourners marched in the twenty-one-mile funeral procession to the city's outskirts. Most of them were dressed in flowing black garb despite the 100-degree heat. Fire trucks sprayed cooling water over the throng, but there was no quelling the mass anguish: The mourners wailed, screamed, and beat themselves on the head and chest. When Khomeini's remains were brought to the burial ground by helicopter, the crowd surged forward, toppling his lidless coffin. Mourners tore pieces from the traditional white Islamic burial shroud, believing it to be divinely blessed. The ayatollah's half-naked body fell out of the coffin and lay in the dust, where it was almost trampled before soldiers were able to regain control. More than 10,000 people were injured in the frenzy. The body, meanwhile, was quickly scooped up by soldiers and returned to the helicopter, which made a hasty takeoff. It returned several hours later, bearing Khomeini's body in a lidded, metal coffin, and the shrouded corpse was moved from the coffin into a waiting grave.

In death, Khomeini remained as ferocious a foe of the West and of Islamic moderation as he had been in life. In his last will and testament, read over the radio while his body lay in state, he denounced his political and religious enemies as "terrorists" and "pirates," then pronounced a final imprecation: "May God's curse be upon them." □

Its shroud slipping, the body of Ayatollah Khomeini spills from its casket as mourners mob his remains during the Iranian leader's 1989 funeral.

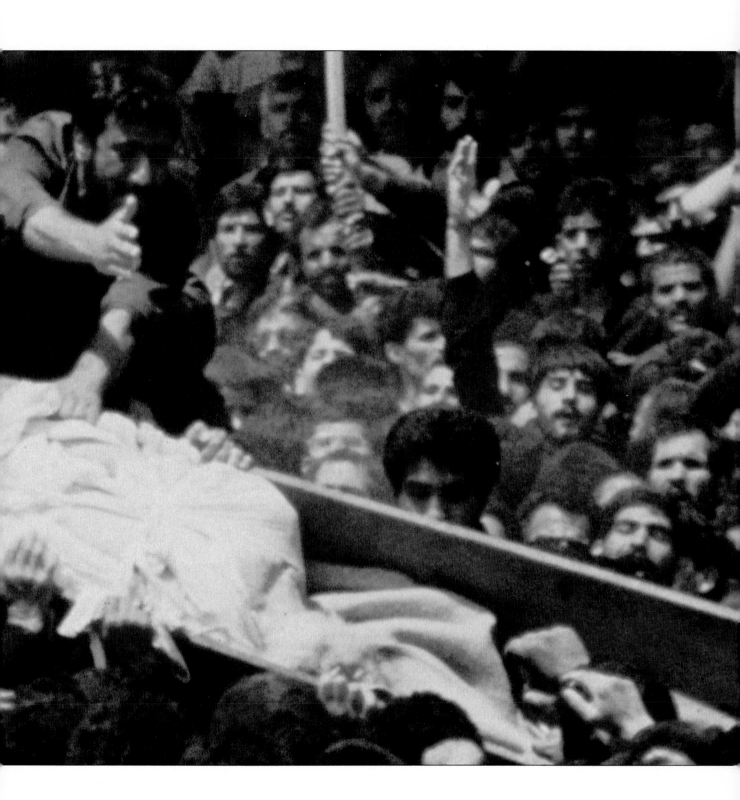

Magical Meals

Food has played a role in funeral rites since the dawn days of humankind—often a supernatural role. Among rural folk, food's function as a magical tool for dealing with the dead lingered well into the modern era: As late as the nineteenth century, for example, Welsh villagers used food to draw off the sins of the deceased. When a person died, relatives called in a specialist known as a sin-eater—typically a loner who lived apart from village society and was suspected of dabbling in witchcraft. A small amount of food was passed to the sin-eater over the body of the departed—or, more rarely, actually placed on the body of the departed—and into the food flowed the guilt of a lifetime's transgressions. The sin-eater devoured this magical meal, taking the guilt into himself and allowing the dead person to enter the hereafter unburdened. Of course the sin-eater himself, laden with all his vicarious evils, was a pariah, shunned by all God-fearing folk. Still, the job had compensations. The sin-eater, usually a very poor person, was at least assured of occasional nourishment.

In the highlands of Bavaria, country people practiced another sort of food magic, their version involving a preparation they called a "corpse cake." After a death, a batch of cake dough was kneaded and then placed on the chest of the deceased to rise. Instead of siphoning off sins, it was thought to absorb the good qualities of the dead person. These virtues remained in the cake when it was baked, and they were passed along to anyone who ate it. □

Last Voyages

Venice is ruled and defined by water—the canals and lagoon and Adriatic expanses that provide the setting for the jewel-like Italian city and dictate unique measures for burying its dead.

Since the early nineteenth century, the municipal cemetery of Venice has been located on the little island of San Michele, which lies to the north of the city and was once the site of a Benedictine monastery. A funeral procession, like so much else in Venice, is thus a journey over water. The city supplies a special boat-hearse to carry the coffin and wreaths. The mourners follow in a line of boats behind.

Venice has always been a magnet for expatriates, and many are buried at San Michele, among them the American poet Ezra Pound and the Russian composer Igor Stravinsky. The 1929 funeral of another Russian, the ballet impresario Sergei Diaghilev, was perhaps the wildest ever held in the island cemetery: One dancer among the mourning throng became so distraught that he leaped into the open grave. □

Golden drapes and urns decorate a mournful black funeral barge making its way down a Venetian canal en route to the island cemetery of San Michele.

The Idol Fallen

With his sculpted features and burning gaze, Rudolph Valentino was Hollywood's premier heartthrob in the early 1920s—"catnip to women," said the acerbic journalist H. L. Mencken. Born Rodolfo Alfonzo Raffaelo Pierre Filibert Guglielmi di Valentina d'Antonguolla in Italy in 1895, he had made his way to the United States at the age of eighteen. He worked as a dishwasher, a gardener, a ladies' escort, and a dancer until a part in *The Four Horsemen of the Apocalypse* propelled him to stardom in 1921. A torrid role in *The Sheik* that same year secured Valentino's status as the screen's great lover. By the time he was thirty-one, in 1926, he had made thirty-four movies, married twice, and demonstrated an epic capacity for nightlife. Then he died.

Valentino's death and its aftermath provided far more drama than any of his films. On August 14, 1926, in a hotel suite in New York, he suddenly fell to the floor, holding his abdomen in agony. The next day, surgeons discovered that he had a perforated ulcer and a ruptured appendix. Peritonitis set in, his temperature soared, and on August 23, his heart stopped.

All over America, women were distraught. At least one committed suicide, shooting herself while clutching her collection of Valentino photographs. (There was grief abroad as well: In London, a woman poisoned herself rather than live with her vicarious loss.) When the actor's body was put on view in a Manhattan funeral chapel, a crowd of 30,000 besieged the place, weeping, screaming, blocking all traffic in the area. The funeral director feared that mourners would pluck jewelry or clothing from the body as souvenirs, so he ordered the casket partially closed, leaving only the actor's head visible. The mourners proceeded to strip the room instead. The next day, the pandemonium continued despite heavy downpours. Another crowd, estimated at 50,000, waited to view the body. Throughout the two-day chaos, police collected scores of wandering children and truckloads of shoes, hats, and umbrellas lost in the fray. Disgusted by the excess, Valentino's manager canceled plans for continuing the public viewing for a whole week. He had the body moved to a more private room in the funeral parlor.

A few days later, the casket was sent west in a locked railroad car. In Chicago, women mobbed the car, many injuring themselves as they tried to break in. The assault did not succeed, but when the train journeyed on to Los Angeles, officials took the sensible precaution of unloading the body at a small station in the suburbs, in order to elude the hysterical assemblage at the main depot.

After a funeral service in Beverly Hills, Valentino went to his last resting place, a mausoleum of Italian marble in Hollywood Cemetery. There was some question as to the whereabouts of his spirit, however. His second wife, who had divorced him, said she had received a message from him through a spirit medium. He was, she said, "in the astral plane and longed to be a legitimate actor"—presumably meaning that a career built on quickening female pulses won no plaudits from critics in the afterlife. □

Marching In

When his health began to decline in his sixties, American jazz great Louis "Satchmo" Armstrong was warned by his physician that blowing the trumpet put a dangerous strain on his heart. "The horn is my life," said the jazzman. "Guess I'll never stop blowing it."

It had been a remarkable life. Born in New Orleans on July 4, 1900, Armstrong grew up in a two-room shack that his family rented for fifty cents a month. He learned to play the cornet while in reform school—he was sent there for shooting a pistol into the air while celebrating New Year's Day of 1913. Once free, he caught the attention of a New Orleans bandleader and rapidly became the most famous figure in jazz, known around the world for his flights of trumpeting genius, growling vocalizations, and his wide and amiable grin.

Death silenced Satchmo in 1971 on July 6, just after his seventy-first birthday, when his failing heart at last gave out. He knew he was dying and hoped he would be given a small, quiet service in New York City, his last home. "Louis was a simple man," said his manager. "He wanted a simple church, simple everything—no music, no sadness."

Things did not turn out that way. As Armstrong lay in state for one day at the Seventh Regiment Armory on Park Avenue in Manhattan, some 25,000 people—of all ages, colors, and social strata—filed past his casket. The funeral itself was attended by 500 people, ranging from old-time musicians to show-business luminaries. Vocalist Peggy Lee sang the Lord's Prayer, and the blind singer Al Hibbler closed with "When the Saints Go Marching In," an Armstrong signature song.

A few days later, a different kind of service was held in New Orleans at the big plaza in front of City Hall. This memorial followed the old tradition for honoring late jazzmen—a doleful march to the cemetery to express the mourning of the living for the dead, then a joyous parade back, celebrating the soul's passage to a better world. In Armstrong's case, both march and parade took place in the plaza. Two brass bands marched slowly to the service, playing dirges and executing their trademark hesitation step. A third band joined in. Mourners and spectators gathered, and eventually a restive crowd estimated at 10,000, sweltering in the humid heat, pressed so close to the speaker's platform that the eulogy had to be canceled. Nonetheless, the past was made present when a New Orleans jazzman blew the haunting notes of taps on Armstrong's childhood cornet. The cornet was then given to a museum, never to be played again. □

Several days after some 25,000 mourning fans filed past the coffin of jazz trumpeter Louis Armstrong in Manhattan's Seventh Regiment Armory (above), Theodore Riley (top) played taps on Armstrong's childhood cornet for a memorial service in New Orleans.

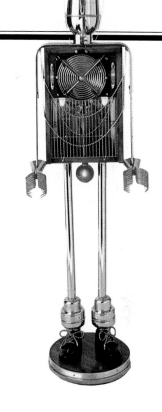

An Artistic Alternative

"Death is like life," says one of the founders of the Ghia Gallery in San Francisco, California. "It can be funny. It can be tragic. It can be hopeful. It can be terrifying. Death is like art." While not everyone would go quite that far, the Ghia Gallery has built a thriving business around an artistic approach to the paraphernalia of death.

Ghia got its start as an outlet for low-cost caskets and urns—a product line that was complemented by free advice about the mortuary industry and how to avoid unnecessary funeral expenses. The gallery owners' jaundiced view of the funeral trade—"an institutionalized system of dealing with death"— prompted an experiment: They invited a number of artists to explore the genre of caskets and urns.

The results, ranging from psychedelic coffins to robotic urns, were provocative, startling, and often beautiful. One urn housed ashes in a truck transmission that had been remodeled to look like a rhinoceros head. Others were created from such objects as a coffee percolator, petrified wood, and an old liquor cabinet that played the song "How Dry I Am." The urn tradition of single occupancy was challenged by a compartmented box designed to hold the ashes of twelve individuals—several generations of a family, suggested the creator, or perhaps twelve friends. The box was surrealistically supported by six pairs of bronze turkey legs. Coffins were painted with abstract designs and constructed out of unusual materials, including biodegradable, recycled paper. Some artists designed wearable jewelry to hold the ashes of loved ones.

Ghia's proprietors see their mission as deinstitutionalizing the American funeral tradition: "We don't take death lightly, nor do we take it too seriously," an owner said, "because death is part of life. Birth and death are both out-of-body experiences." One artist who exhibits at the gallery puts the matter more simply: "For people who like art, what better way to go?" □

Bischof   Herzog   Abt   Ritter   Carthauser   Burgermeister   Domherr

Dancing with Death

On the frescoed wall of the ancient Breton church of La Chaise-Dieu, dancers turn, dip, and sway, raising their arms and bending their knees to the rhythm of unheard music. The richly dressed bishops, princes, and merchants of the troupe mingle with minstrels and common laborers. All step with stately restraint except for the most arresting of all the dancers: the skeletons who throw themselves with wild abandon into the macabre performance, the Dance of Death. The skeletons are reminders that no one, great or lowly, escapes the corruption of the grave. King and peasant alike are destined to be food for worms.

The late Middle Ages was haunted by the dark presence of death. It lurked everywhere, mocking human pretensions and the illusory pleasures of this world. The Dance of Death was a powerful expression of the period's morbid mood: in tapestries, paintings, and stained-glass windows, carved in stone and engraved in metal, corpses in various stages of decay danced the grim fantastic with the living.

The morbid theme was worked and reworked in poetry and drama. In fact, a number of scholars trace the origin of the Dance of Death to a thirteenth-century poem describing three knights who go out hunting and come upon three corpses— their dead selves. The poets were no less graphic about putrefaction than the artists. Wrote one poet: Death makes him shudder and grow pale, / His nose curve, his veins stretch, / His neck swell, his flesh soften, / His joints and tendons grow and strain.

In plays staged before church altars and elsewhere, actors succumbed to death's gruesome embrace, and for a masque that took place in Paris in 1422, men dressed as skeletons danced with players representing every level of society.

Medieval morbidity eventually abated. With the dawn of the Renaissance, an old, comforting idea reasserted itself: In death, the body slips into gentle sleep instead of descending into a nightmare of rotting flesh. But the grim Dance of Death has never ended, and among artists it has never lost its fascination. It saw a revival in nineteenth- and twentieth-century music—the French composer Camille Saint-Saens's *Danse Macabre* is a notable example—and even took a quirky turn in the movies. In the final scene of his film *Love and Death*, for example, Woody Allen capers along a riverbank with the hooded figure of Death. □

Mourning Mementos

In spite of their commitment to building a new and purer society, the settlers of New England brought many a feudal custom across the Atlantic. One was the practice of giving out funeral gifts—scarves, rings, gloves, and other articles. Originally a means of attracting a churchful of people of all classes to pray for the salvation of the depart-ed, funereal gift giving also had social and political overtones. Whether mourners received a gift depended on their closeness to the departed and their social station, and thousands of presents might be dispensed if the deceased were a prominent individual.

Mourning rings were quite popular. Most usually, these were plain gold bands. The bands were deemed more upscale if they were decorated with black or white enamel, but the ones with real cachet were those painted with some sort of appropriate image. In the seventeenth century, skeletons and skulls were popular motifs. A century or so later, the popular scene had softened into a beautiful young woman leaning on an urn beneath a doleful willow tree. Mourning rings that included some of the departed's hair were thought to convey a nice personal touch. Sometimes the hair was braided or twisted to frame an oval painting; sometimes the hair was encased in glass and set into the ring.

Funeral gloves were usually black. They were often given to a broad range of funeral goers, but their quality was apt to vary according to the kinship, social status, or degree of friendship of the mourner. Such distinctions could be a delicate matter and were sometimes worked out in advance: A certain Samuel Fuller of Plymouth specified in his 1663 will that his sister was to receive

gloves costing twelve shillings; Governor Winthrop and his children warranted gloves worth five shillings; and a plebeian acquaintance got a low-grade pair costing a mere two shillings and sixpence.

Over a lifetime, a person could build up a considerable collection of mourning gloves. Andrew Eliot, minister of North Church in Boston, Massachusetts, was awarded 2,940 pairs in thirty-two years; he finally sold the lot for some $650.

By the time of the American Revolution, the cost of funerary largess had become so onerous that some communities passed laws restricting the practice. A Boston statute stipulated that, "to prevent excess and vain expense in mourning," anyone found guilty of giving a gift would be fined twenty shillings. Not everyone was ready to give up the practice, however, and gloves, rings, and the like did not finally fade from the funeral scene until the turn of the last century. □

Various symbols of mourning— angels, urns, skulls, cherubs— and a lock of hair concealed beneath a dark stone graced funereal bracelets and rings in the seventeenth, eighteenth, and early nineteenth centuries.

Museum of Mortality

Anatomist Frederik Ruysch of Amsterdam was brilliant, indefatigable, and single-minded: The structure of the human body fascinated him endlessly. But Ruysch was no dispassionate, hard-headed fact finder. Perhaps influenced by the rampant disease that preyed voraciously on seventeenth-century Europeans, he viewed life and work through the dark lens of a fatalist. In time, he created from the mixed strains of scientific curiosity and gloom an odd kind of public entertainment for his fellow Amsterdamers.

Appointed to a professorship after taking his medical degree, Ruysch practiced his dissection and embalming skills on cadavers by the score—among them, executed criminals and babies found drowned in the city's harbor. He eventually involved his whole family in the business of building up a collection of specimens—skeletons, organs, entire bodies, all exquisitely preserved by drying, embalming, or storage in a fluid whose recipe he never revealed.

Put on display in his house, Ruysch's assemblage presented clinical knowledge in a wrapping of melancholy drama. Preserved infants were dressed in lace garments. Fetuses and skeletons of babies were arranged to form an allegory on life's brevity. Mayflies, flowers, and candles were included in the displays to symbolize transience. Mottoes, proverbs, and other bits of wisdom accompanied the exhibits and added to the dark mood: "Man that is born of women is of few days, and full of trouble"; "Ah Fate, ah Bitter Fate"; ◊

"Time flies and cannot be recalled."

The anatomical museum was a tremendous success, and Ruysch decided to cash in on it; he put it up for sale. There were no takers until Russian czar Peter the Great visited Amsterdam in 1717 and was so impressed with the collection that he bought it for the then-princely sum of 30,000 guilders.

Ruysch promptly applied himself to building up a new and even more doom-steeped collection, dismissing the jibes of scholarly colleagues who thought he was carrying the museum enterprise too far.

To one fellow academic, who declared that such activities were unworthy of a professor, he said, "Come and see." Later, Ruysch noted, "He did not come, but passed into Eternity, just as, to my great convenience, many of my enemies have done equally promptly."

Ruysch himself, so knowledgeable about mortality, did not keep his own appointment with death until he was ninety-three. □

Best Bones

Among the great cities of the world, Paris is a pacesetter in the art of civilized living—and dying, for the Parisian sense of style does not stop at the grave. Nowhere is this more evident than at the cemetery of Père Lachaise, 108 idyllic acres of trees and monuments located on the east side of the city. In its park-like precincts, more than a million people have been buried, among them some of the greatest names in French art, science, and state-craft. Yet Père Lachaise got off to a sluggish start.

The cemetery—located on property that once belonged to Père François d'Aix de La Chaise, confessor to King Louis XIV—was established in the first decade of the nineteenth century to remedy a graveyard crisis. Previously, the city's main burial ground was the Cemetery of the Innocents, a 200-by-400-foot plot that, over a span of eight centuries, had been jammed with two million bodies, stacked atop of one another until the dense

Plants and animals, including this pair of toads, joined the carefully preserved human anatomical specimens in the collection of the anatomist Frederik Ruysch of Amsterdam.

mass of old bones and decaying flesh finally broke though the wall of an adjacent building in a reeking mud slide.

Despite this sickening event, people were slow to accept the alternative of Père Lachaise, even though Napoleon himself had picked out a plot there. Fortunately for the new necropolis, its director, Nicolas Frochot, was a master at marketing, and he set about promoting Père Lachaise as the place to be. To establish the right visual tone, Frochot installed a number of splendid monuments and tombs that had been seized from aristocrats during the French Revolution. And, to lend the grounds instant cultural cachet, he imported the bones of famous people who had been buried elsewhere—French queen Louise de Lorraine, for instance, and medieval lovers Héloïse and Abélard. The great seventeenth-century playwright Molière also ended up at Père Lachaise.

These steps helped, and Père Lachaise did indeed take on the tone of graveyard grandeur to which Frochot had aspired. If any doubt remained, it was dispelled by the enormously popular novelist Honoré de Balzac. As a young man, Balzac found it inspirational to walk through the cemetery's imposing grounds, and as an author, he buried many of his fictional characters at Père Lachaise. The burial scenes occasioned much atmospheric prose from the writer's pen and evidently inspired a number of his readers to plan for burial there as well. So real, in fact, were Honoré de Balzac's fictitious interments that sometimes tourists at Père Lachaise would ask directions to the characters' graves.

In time, Père Lachaise took on unstoppable momentum. The only entry requirements were—and still are—that the applicant was born in Paris, lived in Paris, or died in Paris. As a result, such foreign-born artists as Frederic Chopin, Oscar Wilde, Gertrude Stein, Maria Callas, and the American rock star Jim Morrison can be found at Père Lachaise, sharing the ground with such native luminaries as Eugène Delacroix, Marcel Proust, Edith Piaf, and of course, Honoré de Balzac. Many Parisians would not be caught dead anywhere else. □

Palls and Preparations

When it came to death, Frances Hiller of Wilmington, Massachusetts, believed in having as much splendor as one could afford. And Mrs. Hiller could afford a great deal. In the mid-1870s, her physician husband Henry had begun marketing Elixir, a patent medicine sold as "a revitalizer of youth and energy." Soon rich, Mrs. Hiller persuaded her husband that part of their fortune should go toward the creation of a matching pair of caskets.

Together, they worked out a design. Each casket was to be made of four-inch-thick mahogany, carved with a swirling mix of angels, cupids, dragons, snakes' heads, bats, and other creatures. Inside this casket would be a steel hammock supported by eight brass lions' paws, each seventeen inches tall. The lid was to be decorated with portraits of the couple and their twenty-three children, including seven pairs of twins, who had all supposedly died in infancy (this progeny seems to have been generated solely by Mrs. Hiller's imagination). At the lid's center would be a carving of a skull with a lizard crawling out of one eye socket. Each of the caskets would stand five feet high and weigh some 2,000 pounds.

A local craftsman was hired to execute the containers in a workshop on the Hiller estate. He estimated that, even with the help of four assistants, he would need seven years to complete the job. Dr. Hiller unfortunately died ahead of the craftsman's schedule and had to be stored in a vault for a year until his casket was ready.

After he had been installed and ◊

Under the cherry trees in the garden of the Hillers' Wilmington, Massachusetts, home, workers ready Frances and Henry Hiller's grand mahogany caskets.

placed in a mausoleum in a local cemetery, Mrs. Hiller paid him frequent visits, even though much of her time was consumed by business affairs. She was trying her hand at running the family firm.

Meanwhile, the casket-making team pressed ahead on the second half of the job, and the forward-looking Frances Hiller spent about $20,000 on her funeral robes, which included 500 yards of handmade lace embroidered with thousands of daisies. From time to time, she put

on this terminal attire and got into her casket, critically examining the overall effect in a mirror suspended from the workshop ceiling. She also commissioned a wax model of herself as a stand-in. But Elixir sales were declining, and prefuneral expenditures so depleted the family coffers that Mrs. Hiller put the coffin and robes on exhibit in Boston, charging visitors one dollar for the privilege of viewing her preparations for death.

For all her preoccupation with the hereafter, there were signs that Mrs. Hiller did not find earthly life wholly without appeal. In 1893, she married her coachman, whom the

local newspaper described as "a stolid young Frenchman of apparently little education." It should be noted that she did require him to change his name to Henry Hiller.

Her second marriage notwithstanding, Mrs. Hiller's original burial plan was put into effect when she finally died in 1900 at the age of fifty-five. Ten men, straining mightily before a mass of spectators, maneuvered her remains into position beside the first Henry. The local newspaper commented: "The only events in the little village which attract anywhere near the crowds of today are the annual cattle fairs, and the character of the multitude today was exactly like that which comes yearly to see the prize cattle and have a good time." □

Pet Cemetery

The plaques set flush with the turf in the Rosa Bonheur Memorial Park south of Baltimore bear inscriptions with a distinctive ring: "Pee Wee Daisy, Our Poojums"; "So Silly"; "Little Lady Windy"; "Misty—Sleep softly, my faithful friend." Here, on eight landscaped acres, are buried the remains of more than 28,000 pets, mostly dogs and cats but also rabbits, parakeets, hamsters, squirrels, monkeys, horses, a goat, and an elephant named Mary Ann, who once resided in the Baltimore Zoo.

Named for a nineteenth-century painter of animal portraits, Rosa Bonheur Memorial Park has been the front runner among America's pet cemeteries since its establishment in 1935. It offers undertaking around the clock (pets, like humans, often die at night), and it provides a range of caskets and grave sizes that can cost the pet owners from a few hundred to several thousand dollars. (Although

goldfish are free.) The pet cemetery also supplies special services such as lighting a candle on Christmas, Easter, and the anniversaries of the pet's birth and death. On request, Bonheur will observe Hanukkah and Passover as well. In addition, it provides burial settings tailored to suit the pet—among trees for a dog that liked to run in the woods, near a pool if the animal liked to play in water. At the center of the park is the Tomb of the Unknown Pet; in it lies a stray dog that was found by the cemetery's manager and died soon afterward. The plaque says: "For the millions of lost and abandoned pets, a final resting place."

But the burial ground is not only for pets. Since 1977, humans have been accepted, either in graves beside their pets or in a shared grave. "There's certainly nothing unusual or peculiar about it," says the owner of Rosa Bonheur. "They are just people who love their pets. They loved them in life and continue to love them in death." □

A Kansas Eden

Samuel Perry Dinsmoor was sixty-one years old when he bought a patch of land in the town of Lucas, Kansas, in 1904, but he figured he still had time to make his new home a little paradise. His intentions were more than metaphorical. Over the next two decades, he poured his energies into creating an elaborate limestone house, a companion mausoleum, and an unusual array of statuary designed to represent the Garden of Eden.

The medium for Dinsmoor's Eden was cement, which he worked in various ways into approximate likenesses of trees, plants, and animals, Adam and Eve, the devil, Cain and Abel, and Moses. Perched on cement branches or set beside paths leading through the home-made paradise, the biblical figures embodied their creator's idiosyncratic reading of Scripture. Explaining his depiction of Cain, for example, Dinsmoor wrote: "Moses says ◊

At peace with the pets of his clients, Rosa Bonheur Memorial Park manager Jerry Rosenbaum *(above)* sits among the lamps, flowers, and statues that adorn the grave sites.

wooden boxes will be frying and burning up in the resurrection morn," he explained. "How will they get out when this world is on fire? Cement will not stand fire, the glass will break. This cement lid will fly open and I will sail out like a locust." Until that day arrived, visitors would be welcome at the mausoleum, he said. Everyone except his relatives, however, would have to pay at least one dollar for the privilege of viewing his remains.

Samuel Dinsmoor was in no hurry to go to his final rest. His first wife died in 1917 and seven years later, at the age of eighty-one, he married a twenty-year-old woman and subsequently fathered a child. Dinsmoor continued to live happily in his homemade paradise for another eight years, entering his mausoleum for a permanent stay in his eighty-ninth year. Every year, 10,000 or so visitors pay for a glimpse of Eden and of the embalmed Dinsmoor under glass. □

'Cain was a tiller of the soil,' and he raised great big pumpkins. He is offering a pumpkin. Got hold of the vine pulling it up, but he is trying to hide a hole in the pumpkin with his foot. You see it's a rotten pumpkin. The Lord didn't like rotten pumpkins. I don't blame Him."

Continuing his gloss on Genesis, Dinsmoor said that because Abel's good mutton was more acceptable to God than the rotten pumpkin, Cain killed Abel. "He couldn't have killed him with a gun; they did not have any such implements of warfare in those times, but Cain was a tiller of the soil. I just imagine he got Abel out in the tater patch and brained him with his hoe."

Near his cabin, Dinsmoor erected statues that symbolized the twentieth century—a deeply flawed time, in his personal opinion. Dinsmoor indicated his contempt by populating this section of the yard with sinister representations of bankers, lawyers, and other exploiters of the common man.

Even as he modeled his worldview in concrete, Dinsmoor worked out the details of the mausoleum that would house him when he shed all earthly cares. The crypt was a log-cabin-like structure adorned with a concrete American flag. He also constructed a cement coffin lidded with glass. "It seems to me that people buried in iron and

From 1902 until 1949, the Sears, Roebuck Company catalog featured such mail-order memorials as 1902's tombstones made of "The World's Best Royal Blue Vermont Marble," priced from $5.10 to $26.70, plus the freight charges.

Deathstyles of the Rich and Famous

Among the most famous cemeteries in America is the original Forest Lawn Memorial-Park, 303 rolling acres just eight miles from downtown Los Angeles. One of California's biggest tourist draws, Forest Lawn holds the remains of nearly a century's worth of Hollywood royalty: Clark Gable, Errol Flynn, Humphrey Bogart, Walt Disney, Clara Bow, Jean Harlow, Carole Lombard, Jeanette MacDonald, and many more, not to mention several hundred thousand less celebrated individuals.

Once a tiny, run-down graveyard, Forest Lawn was propelled to cemetery stardom by a hard-selling, Bible-quoting businessman named Hubert Eaton. In a manifesto issued shortly after he arrived to manage the enterprise, Eaton wrote, "I therefore prayerfully resolve on this New Year's Day, 1917, that I shall endeavor to build Forest Lawn as different, as unlike other cemeteries as sunshine is unlike darkness, as Eternal Life is unlike Death." It would be, Eaton went on, "filled with towering trees, sweeping lawns, splashing fountains, singing birds, beautiful statuary, cheerful flow-

ers, noble memorial architecture with interiors full of light and color, and redolent of the world's best history and romances."

Over the years, history and romance were imported or replicated by the ton. Eaton adorned the grounds with the world's largest collection of copies of Michelangelo statuary (plus innumerable other statues that the chronicler Jessica Mitford once described as "the sort of thing one might win in a shooting gallery"). He built a mortuary modeled on a sixteenth-century

English manor house. He erected—for weddings as well as funeral services—a number of likenesses of medieval European churches, including the one that British poet Thomas Gray immortalized in his "Elegy Written in a Country Churchyard." He constructed a museum and filled it with collections of gemstones, ancient coins, and medieval arms and armor. He endowed one building with an immense stained-glass copy of Leonardo da Vinci's *Last Supper*. And he fitted Forest Lawn with gates just like those at Buckingham Palace—but five feet higher and twice as wide.

Although Eaton died in 1966, Forest Lawn has continued to flourish, always faithful to his philosophy of putting history and art to memorial purposes. Four separate Forest Lawn parks, totaling 1,200 acres, are now operating in the Los Angeles area. The newer ones feature such touches of tradition as a mortuary modeled on Mount Vernon, a replica of Boston's Old North Church, and Michelangelo's Sistine Chapel paintings rendered in Venetian glass—all intended, in Hubert Eaton's soaring words, to "remove man's fear of oblivion and bolster his faith in immortality." □

Forest Lawn founder Hubert Eaton and his wife, Anna, lie within the terraced splendor of the cemetery's Great Mausoleum.

Elite's Retreat

In contrast to the imported history featured at Forest Lawn, Moscow's Novo-Devichy Cemetery is deeply rooted in Russia's native past. It is located on the grounds of the Novo-Devichy Convent, a domed complex established in 1524 as a religious retreat for noblewomen—some of whom were locked away in the nunnery because of their unwelcome political views. It became an orphanage under Peter the Great, was looted by Napoleon's soldiers in 1812, served as a prison under the later czars, and was made into a museum by the Communists. After World War II, the government decided to use Novo-Devichy as a cemetery for the nation's elite.

Stalin's first wife was buried there after committing suicide, as was a grandson. It was chosen as the final resting place for one-time premier Nikita Khrushchev and other high-ranking Soviet officials, and it also holds the remains of such cultural icons as the writers Anton Chekhov and Nikolai Gogol and the composers Aleksandr Scriabin and Sergei Prokofiev.

Many monuments at Novo-Devichy were designed to reflect the life's work of the deceased. The grave of World War II tank commander Semen Afonin, for example, is guarded by a one-quarter-size steel replica of a Soviet tank, its gun jutting over a path *(below)*. The achievements of heart surgeon Alexander Nicholaevich Bakulev are symbolically honored by a pair of stone hands *(inset)* holding a three-foot-high heart of red plastic. □

Ice chips flying from their chain saws, a band of chefs compete in an ice sculpting contest at Cedar Park Cemetery near Chicago.

Promotional Pizazz

When Larry Anspach began managing his family's cemetery business in 1973, he wanted to do things differently. Cedar Park, a ninety-three-acre burial ground outside Chicago, had been doing reasonably well ever since his grandfather founded it more than half a century earlier, but Anspach did not like the atmosphere. "I felt if I was going to make a career of this, I had to make it more interesting," he told an interviewer. "This was a pretty morbid place." After a modest first step of installing an aquarium, he proceeded to turn Cedar Park into an arena of activities and attractions that some people likened to Disneyland.

Zestfully promoting his new approach under the motto "Our first concern is for the living," Anspach stocked the grounds with deer, a llama, pheasants, peacocks, swans, and ducks and began offering tours through his outdoor zoo in a tram. He acquired a horse named Elegant Sam to lead funeral processions, planted a banana tree, and built a rock garden. Soon Cedar Park was the scene of many special events: photography contests, Easter-egg hunts, pumpkin-decorating contests, Christmastime visits by Santa Claus, and an annual ten-kilometer run dubbed Heaven Can Wait.

As a marketer, Anspach did not miss a trick. For a time, he offered $200 coupons to be applied to funeral expenses, gave $50 discounts when the Chicago Bulls basketball team scored more than 100 points in a game, and won a reputation for public service by offering free burials for organ donors, free graves for reformed drug addicts or victims of handguns, and free funerals and burials for people who had been killed by drunk drivers.

In 1991, Larry Anspach sold the business, and the new owners opted for a lower profile. But he had made his point: "Just because we're a cemetery," he once said, "doesn't mean we should hide in a corner." □

Houses of the Dead

The custom of equipping the dead with material goods for use in the afterlife was once widespread. The ancient Egyptians, most notably, provided all sorts of comforts for their corpses. Ancient Scythians even went so far as killing servants and pets so that the departed could have company in the next world. The tradition has waned in modern times, of course, but it has not vanished. Note the East Serbian region of Yugoslavia, where, by the late 1970s, a flourishing free market for farm products had given many peasants the wherewithal to write a new chapter in the old story of grave goods.

With their excess cash, the people began erecting nicely furnished houses above or near the gravesites of their loved ones.

The grave houses were inspired by an ancient pagan belief that Serbia's Orthodox Church has never rooted out: The living need to provide for the dead, both to curry their favor and to help them find the way to the nether world. Ignoring the dead invites their anger and, as a consequence, a ruined crop or some other vengeful bit of bad luck.

The grave house is usually a two-room affair: a concrete basement that houses the coffin, and a furnished room at ground level. The upstairs "living" quarters may contain chairs, a stove, a refrigerator, utensils, magazines, items especially treasured by the deceased in life, even up-to-the-minute appliances such as VCRs. The comforts are not necessarily for the exclusive use of the departed. Relatives and friends may gather there to talk, enjoy a meal, share a drink, or play cards. However convivial the gathering, though, the departed one is not forgotten. Over the door of the grave house of a young man killed during a visit to France are engraved these words: "Because of Paris, which took my life, my parents are shedding tears." □

Live plants, a parquet floor, and a polished stone memorial grace the dining room of a grave house in Dublje, Yugoslavia (above), while roses adorn the exterior of another (left) in the village cemetery of nearby Markovac.

they could not dig up the dead, they would do in the living.

The most notoriously successful of this ghoulish breed were William Burke and William Hare, a pair of Irish petty crooks living in Edinburgh in 1827. Hare had taken over a cheap rooming house by moving in with its widowed owner, and Burke and his mistress were among the lodgers. When an elderly resident died owing four pounds' back rent, Hare decided to sell the corpse in order to pay the debt. He got Burke to help. Together they opened the old man's coffin, removed the body, replaced it with trash, and sold the cadaver to

Knox's anatomy school for the sum of seven pounds, ten shillings. The sale, which covered the debt and turned a profit besides, exceeded Hare's expectations.

From there it was but a short and logical step from resurrectionist to executioner. When another lodger fell ill, Burke and Hare smothered him with a pillow. An old beggar woman was invited in for a friendly drink, then suffocated as she awoke from a drunken stupor. The bodies of these victims and others were delivered to Dr. Knox at ten pounds apiece. Combing the poor quarters of Edinburgh for additional prey, Burke and Hare dispatched at least sixteen of the aged and down-and-out over the next year before suspicious lodgers at their rooming house summoned the police. Officials arrested Burke and Hare and raised pointed

questions about Knox's role in the killings. Apparently satisfied that the doctor had not instigated the murders, police did not charge him. But the gossip ruined Knox, and he never taught anatomy again. Hare was acquitted after testifying that the scheme was Burke's idea. Burke was hanged on January 28, 1829, but his punishment did not end there. The judge ordered that his body follow the path of his victims: It was to be "publicly dissected and anatomised," and, after that, its skeleton was to be preserved and exhibited as a testament to the infamous resurrectionist's atrocities. The sentence was carried out, and Burke's bones remain on display in the anatomical museum of the University of Edinburgh. □

The Harrison Horror

In America, as in Europe, medical students in the early nineteenth century found it hard to get cadavers on which to hone their surgical skills. There were few legitimate sources of bodies, so graverobbing was epidemic wherever medical schools flourished. More than a few American families—the great as well as the lowly—were victimized by resurrectionists, but perhaps none suffered so shockingly or publicly as did the Harrisons of Indiana and Ohio in 1878.

On May 26 of that year, seventy-three-year-old John Scott Harrison died at his home in North Bend, Ohio, near Cincinnati. Harrison was a member of a large and prominent family. A former congressman, he was the last surviving son of William Henry Harrison, the ninth U.S. president, and the father of General Benjamin Harrison, who would become the twenty-third president of the United States. Following a well-attended funeral, this son and father of presidents was buried near his own father in the family plot at North Bend.

Buried nearby was John Scott Harrison's recently deceased grandnephew, Augustus Devin; and to John Scott's mourners, Devin's grave appeared to have been recently disturbed. Sure enough, a search revealed an empty coffin where Devin should have lain. After posting watchmen to stand guard over the grave of John Scott, family members and policemen led by John Harrison—son of John Scott and brother of president-to-be Benjamin Harrison—went searching for Devin's stolen remains. John Harrison hoped that he could restore Devin's corpse to its resting place without the young man's mother ever learning of the theft.

John Harrison and his investigators went immediately to the Ohio Medical College in Cincinnati. There they discovered a cloth-shrouded corpse—presumably Devin's—hanging by its neck at the end of a rope in an air shaft below the school's dissecting room. When the shroud was removed, however, John Harrison was confronted not with Devin's face, but that of his own father, the just-buried John Scott Harrison. Guards notwithstanding, the grave in North Bend had been ransacked the day after the old man's burial.

As soon as the elder Harrison's remains were reburied in the secure vault of a family friend, the search continued for Devin's body. The Harrisons' inquiries revealed that Cincinnati had become a midwestern shipping hub for dissectible corpses, and through its routes Devin's body had made its way to a morgue in Ann Arbor, Michigan. At last, four weeks after its first burial, the young man's body was reinterred in the family plot in Ohio.

Although two men were indicted, no one was convicted for stealing the bodies. Two years after John Scott Harrison's death, however, Ohio passed new laws that set harsh penalties for body snatching and warned medical schools to use strictly legitimate avenues to obtain cadavers for study. □

Haunted President

In life, President Abraham Lincoln was haunted by images of death. In death, Lincoln was haunted by the ghoulish and greedy living.

A week before his assassination, Lincoln dreamed of entering the East Room of the White House, where he saw a corpse laid out in a casket. The president related the dream to his family as follows: " 'Who is dead in the White House?' I demanded of one of the soldiers. 'The President,' was his answer. 'He was killed by an assassin!' "

Lincoln was shot once in the head by John Wilkes Booth on the evening of April 14, 1865, and he died the next morning. The Army Medical Museum in Washington retained seven shards of skull torn out by the fatal bullet. These fragments, a few strands of hair, and the attending surgeon's shirt cuffs, stained with the president's blood, are still preserved by the museum, which is now called the National

Museum of Health and Medicine.

After lying in state in Washington and then traveling across a grieving country to Springfield, Illinois, on a military funeral train, Lincoln's body was interred in a vault in Oak Ridge Cemetery.

Eleven years later, members of a counterfeiting gang broke into the tomb, hoping to steal the president's body and ransom it for some $200,000 and the release of one of their comrades from the Illinois state prison. The outlaws had partially removed the casket from its sarcophagus when they were interrupted by Secret Service agents. The agents had been alerted by a gang member who was in reality a Pinkerton undercover detective. The would-be body snatchers escaped but were arrested the following night. No law prohibited body stealing at that time, and the men were jailed for a year for attempted larceny and conspiracy.

After the incident, the president's son, Robert Todd Lincoln, took measures to see that his father would henceforth rest undisturbed. In accordance with the son's wishes, the remains of Abraham Lincoln were interred at Oak Ridge in a vault ten feet below ground. He remains there today. His sarcophagus is encased in a concrete jacket. Nearby in the same vault are the bodies of his wife, Mary Todd Lincoln, and the three Lincoln sons. □

Abraham Lincoln's body, encased in concrete, is impervious to thieves. His few relics include a life mask *(left)*, strands of his hair *(top)*, and the bloodstained shirt cuffs of a surgeon who attended him.

Trampled Rest

For a while after his death, Charlie Chaplin's final resting place was neither final nor restful. On December 27, 1978, the British comic legend was buried in a cemetery near his home in the quaint Swiss hamlet of Coursier-sur-Vevey. Chaplin would surely have enjoyed the view from the graveyard: the magnificent Swiss and French Alps and the splendor of Lake Geneva. But on March 1, 1979, the view changed drastically. Chaplin's body, inside a heavy oak coffin, was unceremoniously snatched from the ground, dragged past the villagers' modest headstones and over a low stone wall and off into the moonlit night. All that was left was a gaping hole that townspeople discovered the next morning.

As Swiss police sought the culprits, rumors spread. One version of events was that overzealous British fans had returned the body to London, where the talented actor had kicked off his career in music halls and mime troupes seventy years earlier. Another account accused Jewish fanatics of exhuming Chaplin, who was Jewish, to perform a proper Orthodox burial. But some interpretations were less dire. Swiss newspaper headlines wondered if this was somehow "the final gag of Chaplin's astonishing career."

With less whimsy, magistrate Jean-Daniel Tenthorey alerted the international police agency Interpol to a likely plot of "madmen, fanatics, or miscreants trying to make money" by extorting a ransom from Chaplin's widow, Oona, who was principal heir to his vast estate.

Sure enough, several weeks after Chaplin's casket disappeared, Oona Chaplin received a telephone call demanding $600,000 for the return of the body. She refused to pay. More conversations followed, and the widow negotiated ever-lower ransoms. By the time the asking price was reduced to $125,000, police had tapped the Chaplin phone lines and staked out 200 telephone booths in the region. When the robbers called to make final ransom arrangements, police traced the call and nabbed the graverobbers at a public phone in Lausanne. The culprits turned out to be an unemployed Polish auto mechanic named Roman Wardas and his Bulgarian sidekick, Galtscho Ganev. Charged with attempted extortion and "disturbing the peace of the deceased," the bungling body burglars confessed that they had loaded Chaplin's corpse into the back of a car and carried it fifteen miles to a makeshift grave site in an unsuspecting farmer's cornfield.

Because the thieves could not remember where in the cornfield they had buried Chaplin, investigators used a mine detector to recover the coffin. Chaplin's body, unharmed, was reinterred in a concrete vault at his original burial site. □

Conquered

William I, the Norman duke who subdued England at the Battle of Hastings and became its king in 1066, was known by his court as the Conqueror. But commoners were less awed by the king's remote majesty. They focused not on William's greatness, but on his girth, dubbing him "the fat man" and mocking him for appearing to be pregnant.

Indeed, this was not the only indignity borne by the hero of Hastings. William, born to his father's mistress, was also known as William the Bastard. But the most inglorious moment of William's life came not at its beginning, but at its end.

In the summer of 1087, as the king journeyed to a spa in Rouen, the capital of Normandy, his horse reared up and shoved its iron saddle horn into William's prodigious paunch, rupturing his intestines. A raging infection followed, subjecting the monarch to five weeks of intense pain, nausea, and vomiting, and, finally, death.

At the end, William's already capacious midsection was grotesquely bloated by disease. It swelled still more in the summer heat—so much so that by the time of his funeral in a chapel at Caen, the clergy and mourners were unable to fit the royal body into its sarcophagus: The casket was too narrow and too short as well.

Subjected to continued pushing and squeezing, the royal cadaver burst, spewing putrefaction in all directions. Mourners raced from the chapel to escape the overwhelming stench, the service was cut short, and the king's exploded remains were hastily and unceremoniously interred. □

Once Honored, Twice Buried

The bodies of the distinguished dead are often moved from one burial place to another, as the living change their notion of what constitutes a fitting memorial. But the remains of General Anthony Wayne, hero of the American Revolution, own a singular distinction: They rest in two different graves.

One of George Washington's ablest officers, Wayne earned the sobriquet Mad Anthony for his reckless but triumphant assaults on the British and, later, on the Indians whom he helped drive from Ohio. Wayne took sick and died on December 15, 1796, at Fort Presque Isle, which later became part of Erie, Pennsylvania. In accord with his wishes, the general was given a soldier's burial at the foot of the flagpole beside the fort's blockhouse on Garrison Hill.

This fairly conventional arrangement lasted thirteen years. But in 1809, Wayne's son, Colonel Isaac Wayne, arrived in Erie proposing to return his father's remains to Radnor, Pennsylvania, so he could lie with other family members in the family cemetery by St. David's Episcopal Church. Expecting that the general's grave would by then yield nothing but bones, Colonel Wayne had undertaken his mission in a sulky, a light, two-wheeled, one-horse carriage. To the son's surprise, however, the father's body emerged from the ground nearly intact (the chemical makeup of the soil had helped preserve it) and far too bulky and heavy to be carried on a sulky. Rather than hire a wagon to carry the entire body, the colonel seems to have struck upon the notion of reducing his father's corpse to a more transportable size. For this he turned to Dr. J. C. Wallace, an army surgeon who had served with the senior Wayne. Wallace separated the general's bones from his flesh in a toilsome procedure that involved some surgery and some boiling of various parts in a large kettle. The colonel came to regret his decision, writing that, had ◊

A portrait of General Anthony Wayne pokes from the three-foot-wide kettle that was used to boil his remains. Similar pots were used to make soap and maple syrup at the time.

he known what the doctor would do to his father's remains, "I should certainly have had them again deposited there and let them rest."

But bones were what Wayne had gone for, and bones were what he eventually got. Packing the skeletal remnants onto his sulky, the colonel returned home and reburied his father as planned. Meanwhile, the

doctor laid Anthony Wayne's flesh and entrails back in the coffin, along with the dissecting tools that had been used on the body. The remaining bits of the general were then reinterred beside the blockhouse in Erie.

For a time, Garrison Hill ceased to be regarded as Wayne's grave, although a local historian maintained that "more in weight and more in bulk was reinterred in the Erie grave than was taken away." The blockhouse burial site was neglected; the building was even used as a cowshed before being burned by some vandals.

It fell to another physician, an antiquarian named Edward W. Germer, to redress this neglect. In

1875, Germer uncovered a decayed wood-and-leather coffin on the site; driven into the lid were a number of brass tacks, arranged so they spelled out: "A.W. / Ob. Dec. 15, / 1796." This legend, together with the dissecting utensils remaining within the casket, convinced Germer that he had found the grave of the flesh, if not the bones, of Mad Anthony Wayne. Germer crusaded for proper marking of the general's first place of burial—now considered his principal grave—and eventually managed to have a faithful replica of the old military blockhouse built on the site. The coffin lid and the dissecting tools became part of an Anthony Wayne museum in the new structure. □

Death of a Vampire

Bela Lugosi, perhaps the most rigidly typecast actor in Hollywood history, took his most famous role with him to the grave. A serious performer who had played in the dramas of Shakespeare and Ibsen in his native Hungary, Lugosi built his American career on his silkily sinister portrayal of Count Dracula, the legendary Transylvanian vampire.

First on Broadway and then in the 1931 film *Dracula*, Lugosi chilled audiences with his rendering of the aristocratic bloodsucker. The actor's menacing dark eyes and exotic accent suited the role; on screen he was deliciously evil. Lugosi went on to appear in other parts in dozens of horror movies, but he seemed always mindful that Dracula was his singular creation, the role he wore as distinctively and elegantly as he did the count's characteristic opera cloak.

Lugosi died in 1956, aged seventy-three, still very much in the character of his alter ego. He was buried in Holy Cross Cemetery at Inglewood, California. At his own request, the actor went to his coffin the way Count Dracula had always gone to his: in full evening dress, cloak and all. □

Bela Lugosi poses as his alter ego, the menacing vampire Count Dracula.

Evita on Tour

In life and in death, Argentina's Eva Duarte de Perón was the stuff of legend. She was born illegitimate and poor—but not without certain assets: She was beautiful, crafty, relentlessly determined, and short on scruples. With those armaments, she managed to claw her way up from squalid anonymity to become, at the age of twenty-six, one of the most powerful women in the world.

Eva Duarte began her career as an actress, and as such she was distinctly mediocre. But she did have a knack for self-promotion and an unfailing ability to seek out and attract powerful men. Making her way profitably from protector to protector, she eventually encountered Colonel Juan Perón and became his mistress and later his wife.

Evita, as she came to be known to the world, was scorned by the powerful upper and middle classes of her country as hopelessly common. In response, she cleverly turned her humble origins to good advantage, rallying the masses of poor Argentine peasants and laborers to Juan Perón's cause. As a result, the young colonel made his way through the shadowy, perilous ranks of Argentine politics and in 1946 became the country's president and absolute ruler. And Evita, championing the rights of the downtrodden, kept his power base firmly in place. The Peróns ruled ruthlessly, intimidating or eliminating their enemies. They also grew rich, stashing vast wealth in ◊

numbered Swiss bank accounts. Even so, among her *descamisados*—"shirtless ones"—Evita achieved a status somewhere between stardom and sainthood.

Probably, Juan and Eva Perón loved each other. Certainly, they both loved power. Thus when Evita died of cancer in 1952 at the age of only thirty-three, Juan Perón suffered a double loss: a cherished wife and the power that she represented. The Argentine dictator set out to preserve what he could of both.

After her death on July 26, Evita's body lay in state in the Ministry of Labor in Buenos Aires for two weeks; some two million mourners paid their respects. The ensuing funeral was on a scale normally reserved for Argentine heads of state. The widower then made plans to have Evita's body displayed in a public mausoleum. She was embalmed in a yearlong, $100,000 process—roughly that used to preserve Vladimir Lenin's remains in Moscow—in which her blood was gradually replaced with alcohol, then glycerin, and her skin was coated with plastic. The embalming virtually ruled out any chance of dehydration and decay. Thus preserved, Evita's body was returned to the Central Labor Building while preparations were made for a grand final entombment. But before that could take place, the dictator was overthrown in a 1955 coup.

Evita, whose posthumous presence had helped keep her husband in power, now threatened those who had deposed him. On the night of December 22, 1955, her body disappeared, stolen by anti-Perónists who wanted to remove from view this most potent symbol of Perónist appeal. But while the graverobbers sought to get the corpse out of the public view, they also knew that they could not afford to destroy it, lest word of such a desecration leak out and excite the wrath of millions of Evita's worshipers.

Thus, Evita Perón became one of history's best-traveled cadavers, although the story of her rovings is scrambled. Some say that her coffin was sealed in a packing crate marked "RADIO SETS" and shuffled for a time among various offices and warehouses in Rio de Janeiro. It is certain that the macabre package was briefly stored at the Argentine embassy in Bonn, Germany, before being moved to Rome. In 1957, Evita was secretly buried in Milan.

Her body lay there in peace until 1971, when the Argentine government—in what it called an "act of Christian dignity"—had it delivered to Juan Perón, who was living in Madrid and married to his third wife, Isabel. When the coffin lid was raised, Perón burst into tears, exclaiming, "She is not dead, she is only sleeping!" Except for a flattened nose, the mummified corpse was in a remarkable state of preservation. Perón reburied Evita in a crypt in Madrid, vowing he would one day take her home.

Two years later, the turning tide of politics swept Juan Perón back into power in Argentina, but he failed to share his triumphal return with Evita. Perón died a year later.

His widow, Isabel, succeeded him as president and promptly brought home the corpse of Evita. By then the long-dead heroine was a cult figure, and her presence once again bolstered the fortunes of a living Perón. □

A mourner swears undying loyalty to the orchid-framed body of Eva Perón, wife of dictator Juan Perón, as other grieving citizens pay their last respects to Argentina's beloved Evita.

Curtain Call

Opera legend Enrico Caruso gave his last stage performance on Christmas Eve in 1920, singing the role of Nemorino in Donizetti's *L'Elisir d'Amore* at the Brooklyn Academy of Music in New York. He died eight months later at the age of forty-eight from peritonitis.

Although the great Italian tenor's voice was no longer heard, he continued to perform for his followers, after a fashion, for several years. After his death, Caruso's body was placed in a transparent crystal casket and put on public display in a chapel at the Santa Maria del Pianto cemetery near Naples, Italy, the singer's birthplace.

Caruso, always a stylish dresser, remained as fashionable in death as he had been in life: Fellow tenor Tito Schipa and other friends provided the embalmed corpse with a new, up-to-date change of clothes each year. Finally, after Caruso had been on exhibit for six years, his widow grew weary of the macabre vigils that fans held at her husband's grave. She ordered a slab of white granite placed over the casket and had the mausoleum locked. Enrico Caruso has not entertained an audience since. □

Photographs and flowers flanked by classical pillars decorate the grand chapel and marble sarcophagus housing the remains of operatic great Enrico Caruso.

Sixteenth-century artist Martin van Heemskerck created this image of the grand but probably never-occupied tomb of Mausolus in Halicarnassus.

Living Memorial

Mausolus, a ruler of the ancient land of Caria in present-day Turkey, died in 353 BC. His reign was unexceptional, but his tomb was so grand that the king's name lives on in a modern word for a magnificent tomb, *mausoleum*. His widow, Artemisia—who was also his sister—built the monument at Halicarnassus, where Bodrum, Turkey, now stands. The three-tiered edifice, featuring works by the greatest sculptors of the day, was topped by a heroic statue of Mausolus in a chariot drawn by four horses. The structure became one of the Seven Wonders of the ancient world.

Ironically, Mausolus himself probably never rested there. Legend has it that Artemisia dissolved her husband-brother's ashes in perfumed water and drank him down—making her, not the grand edifice, the first mausoleum. □

When the teak coffin arrived at the Aspin Hill Pet Cemetery in Maryland, it was accompanied by a request: "Please give Pesky a decent burial. We have enjoyed his company for three years." The coffin held a dead fly. The cemetery complied with its clients' wishes.

Beauty in Bone

In a city of magnificent churches, Rome's Santa Maria della Concezione stands out. Beneath its nave lies an underground corridor 130 feet long. Arches divide the subterranean hallway into six vaulted chambers. Chandeliers hang from the ceiling. The walls are elaborately decorated in floral patterns. The quality and detail of the work are exceptional—all the more so for the material used: Every item is crafted of human bones. Pelvic bones form the chandeliers; interlaced ribs describe stars; femurs and fibulae construct elaborate curlicues. Skulls abound, and throughout the display sit the mummified bodies of monks fully garbed in their modest vestments.

The vaulted tunnel is, in fact, neither church nor museum, but the cemetery of the Capuchin friars who have operated this and many other churches in Italy for centuries. Between 1528 and 1870, the cemetery accumulated the remains of some 4,000 friars. Then interment stopped and decoration began—using the remains of the departed. The work, said to have been designed by an unnamed French friar, is intended to be the Capuchins' "monument to death and hymn of resurrection," according to the church's guidebook. □

A winged hourglass symbolizing death overlooks mummified Capuchin friars whose bodies attest to the fate of all flesh. Surrounding the mummies are mystical images constructed of skulls and bones. Their chamber is one of six beneath Rome's church of Santa Maria della Concezione.

Remembrance of Things to Come

For nearly three centuries, the wealthy of Palermo, Sicily, were interred just outside the city in the catacombs below the church of the Capuchin monastery of Zita. But this place of final rest was built more for the living than the dead. The Capuchin friars who maintained it called it a *memento mori*—a vivid reminder to the living that they, too, would one day die.

More than 8,000 mummified remains populate the catacombs beneath the monastery *(below)*. Withered bodies of men and women sit, stand, and recline rigidly. Many appear to have been frozen in their final earthly moments, their eyes wide, mouths gaping, and faces twisted, leaving the living to speculate whether their last visions were of ecstasy or horror. Remnants of clothing still cling to some of the torsos. Fragments of skull peek from behind shriveled flesh. Against one wall is an altar assembled from human skulls, inlaid with a mosaic of human teeth. The dust of centuries covers all.

The necropolis began in the early seventeenth century as the final resting place of the monastery's friars. Later, until it ceased being used in 1881, Zita became the fashionable place of interment for the rich and famous of Palermo. The tombs even contain the remains of a king of Tunis. Each body underwent a thorough mummification before being put in its permanent resting place. And once positioned, the new resident had a name tag placed around its neck so that families of the deceased could return to contemplate their loved ones. □

Mummy Dummy

In December of 1976, a Universal Studios camera crew arrived at the Nu-Pike Amusement Park in Long Beach, California, to film an episode of the popular television action series "The Six Million Dollar Man." Preparing the scene in a corner of the park's fun house, the crew encountered a typical house of horrors prop—a body, painted with ghastly red phosphorescent paint, dangling from the end of a rope. Trouble began when a worker moved the body. An arm came off, and inside it was a human bone.

This was no dummy, but a mummy—in fact, a man with a bullet wound in his chest and so much embalming arsenic in his veins that his brain and heart had become as hard as stone. Inside the mummy's mouth were two clues to his identity: a 1924 penny and a ticket stub from "Louis Sonney's Museum of Crime, So. Main St., L.A." Since the man had obviously met a violent end, Los Angeles police began a murder investigation. What they eventually uncovered was the bizarre trail of one of the last Wild West badmen.

The body was that of Elmer McCurdy, a young man who began and ended his criminal career in 1911. The end came in Oklahoma, where McCurdy stopped a train and made off with just forty-six dollars and two jugs of whiskey. The outlaw drank the whiskey, then imprudently announced to a sheriff's posse that he would not be taken alive. He was not.

Although McCurdy's criminal career had been of short duration, his corpse began a prolonged odyssey through the world of carnivals and Wild West shows. Appropriately, he played the part of a former desperado.

McCurdy's post-mortem career began when the sheriff whose posse had killed him took the corpse to Pawhuska, Oklahoma. There an undertaker named Joseph L. Johnson measured, photographed, and embalmed it, then dressed it in a cowboy hat and six-guns. With McCurdy looking pretty good for a cadaver, Johnson leaned him in a corner of the back room and charged the locals a nickel to see "The Bandit Who Wouldn't Give Up." The nickels were dropped into McCurdy's open mouth, from which Johnson retrieved them from time to time. Photographers made postcards of the train robber.

Carnival promoters passing through town offered to buy McCurdy and exhibit him, but the undertaker decided to hold on to the holdup man until the next of kin claimed him. After all, McCurdy was providing steady revenue.

In 1915, two men arrived as- ◊

Before his body undertook its sixty-year carnival tour, outlaw Elmer McCurdy was photographed in a coffin shortly after a sheriff shot and killed him near Pawhuska, Oklahoma, in 1911.

A traveling photographer snapped this tintype of Billy the Kid in 1879, a year before Pat Garrett shot the outlaw down in Lincoln County, New Mexico.

serting that the corpse was that of their long-lost brother. They hauled the body away, headed for their home in California, they said, to give their sibling "a decent burial." In fact, the "brothers" were carnival promoters, and soon the well-preserved robber joined show business in earnest. He appeared in a street carnival in Texas. He made rounds in circus sideshows, billed as "The Outlaw Who Would Never Be Captured Alive." He popped up in Arizona and in the early 1920s was part of an Oklahoma road show. At various times, McCurdy graced a haunted house at an amusement park near Mount Rushmore in South Dakota and laid in an open casket at a wax museum in Los Angeles. He had been hanging from a beam in the Long Beach fun house for about four years before Hollywood's Bionic Man almost gave him his biggest role ever.

The police investigation that uncovered these details of Elmer McCurdy's peripatetics put an end to the exhibitions. But it could not prevent McCurdy from attracting one last audience. On a rainy Friday morning in April of 1977, hundreds of spectators lined the route to Summit View Cemetery in Guthrie as the last cowboy outlaw to be buried in Oklahoma's red soil was laid to rest. To make sure that the corpse would not turn up again, the state medical examiner ordered two cubic yards of concrete to be poured over the coffin before the grave was closed. □

Carving Up Billy

Billy the Kid won notoriety during his brief lifetime as a cattle rustler, killer, and braggart. Although few who knew his viperous personality sought his friendship while he lived, in death the Kid became the object of cultlike veneration. He became, in fact, a sort of collector's item.

Born William H. Bonney in New York City in 1859, the unruly Kid bragged in 1880 that he had killed at least twenty-one men in New Mexico, Arizona, and Colorado—one victim for every year of his young life. But before his twenty-second birthday, he was dead himself, shot through the heart by his former friend Sheriff Pat Garrett.

Not long after Bonney's demise, numerous promoters and swindlers were exhibiting what they billed as "Billy the Kid's Genuine Exhumed Remains" to a gullible public. Most of these entrepreneurs boasted of personally stealing the body from its resting place at New Mexico's Fort Sumner Military Cemetery. Had their claims been true, the exhumation would have been a crowded event, for "genuine corpses" of Billy the Kid were as common as the sideshows that wandered the West.

Nevertheless, tickets were sold far and wide to eager throngs, who usually wound up viewing anonymous corpses tricked up to look like Billy. Business was not diminished even by the protestations of Pat Garrett, who wrote a biography of Billy two years after killing him, and in it insisted that the Kid's body had never left its grave. "And I speak of what I know," Garrett added ominously. □

Sculptor Korczak Ziolkowski put the finishing touches on the seven-ton granite bust of Sitting Bull shortly before it was installed over the Sioux shaman's grave and memorial in Mobridge, South Dakota.

Roving Bull

Although he was more medicine man than warrior, Sitting Bull led the last Sioux Indian resistance to the white man's invasion of the South Dakota territory during the last half of the nineteenth century. Agents of the United States government killed both Sitting Bull and his cause in 1890. But the memory of the Sioux leader endured, and six decades after his death, Sitting Bull became the subject of interstate contention and the prize in an elaborate body-snatching caper.

In December of 1890, at the age of fifty-nine, Sitting Bull was one of fourteen Sioux killed in a battle with Indian police employed by the federal government. The battle was fought at the great shaman's home on the Grand River near the present town of Mobridge, South Dakota. Arriving late on the scene, U.S. cavalrymen carted his body forty miles from Mobridge to Fort Yates, North Dakota. He was buried without ceremony near the fort's cemetery. In 1903, the army closed the fort and transferred the remains of soldiers in its cemetery to a new resting place in Iowa. The corpse of Sitting Bull went too, but local Sioux protested, and his coffin was reinterred in the town of Fort Yates.

The government covered the grave with a concrete slab, but otherwise the little graveyard, with Sitting Bull its lone occupant, remained undisturbed and neglected under the auspices of the U.S. Department of the Interior.

Almost fifty years passed. Then, in 1952, some white residents of Mobridge joined forces with Sitting Bull's nephew and three granddaughters and hatched a plan to establish a memorial to the great shaman near the South Dakota site where he died. The townspeople of Fort Yates objected, apparently reasoning that Sitting Bull's grave honored the town, even if the town did not noticeably honor the grave. Nevertheless, the fallen hero's kin persuaded the Interior Department to relinquish Sitting Bull's body, and preparations for the move began.

Working in secret to avoid interference from Fort Yates citizens, the South Dakotans converged on the burial plot at four o'clock one snowy winter morning, bringing with them a truck with a power hoist to raise the concrete slab, a crew of diggers, three getaway cars, a box to hold the shaman's bones, and a steel vault that would house the remains once they returned to Mobridge. Soon the team had retrieved Sitting Bull's bones, photographed them, placed them in their box, and set the box in the steel vault. Then the South Dakotans scanned the still-dark sky for the airplane that would fly the vault to Mobridge.

But weather had grounded the plane, so the group was forced to beat a retreat toward the South Dakota border. To foil any interference, the bones were transferred from the vault to one of the cars, and each of the three cars followed a separate route home. The large vault, openly displayed in the back of a pickup truck to decoy any possible ▷

pursuers, took yet another route.

Shortly after dawn, the conspirators converged on a parcel of South Dakota land overlooking the Missouri River, a plot that had just been christened Dakota Memorial Park. A power shovel scooped out a grave ten feet deep, and a ready-mix truck poured a two-foot-deep bed of concrete. Sitting Bull's bones, returned once more to the steel vault, were lowered into the hole and covered with more concrete. By the time the people of Fort Yates awoke to learn that Sitting Bull's bones were gone, the remains lay snugly within a twenty-ton block of concrete south of the state border.

The body snatching made the front pages of newspapers across the country, giving the new tomb a head start as a successful tourist attraction. When it opened officially in September 1953, Sitting Bull's grave was topped by a seven-ton granite bust and surrounded by an iron fence. □

Lasting Tan

On a spring day in 1950, two Danish farmers were cutting peat in a drained bog called Tollund Fen when they encountered the body of a man. When the creased brow, stubbled chin, and unseeing eyes emerged from the black earth, the man's face reportedly displayed a distinctive nobility and gentleness. Suspecting that they had found the victim of a recent murder, the farmers called the police. But there would be no criminal investigation, no manhunt. Although the man in the bog had indeed been killed, there had probably

been no crime. And even if there had been, there were no suspects to prosecute. Tollund Man, as he became known, had been dead for some 2,000 years.

Despite its age, the corpse was nearly intact, missing only some skin from the left shoulder and the chest. This Iron Age relic had been preserved by the acid-rich waters of the bog, which tanned the flesh in the same way that chemicals tan leather.

The man was clad only in belt and pointed cap, both made of animal hide. A noose of twisted thongs around his neck told researchers that Tollund

Dignified and graceful in death, the acid-tanned preserved head of Tollund Man rests in the Silkeborg Museum of Central Jutland, a scant six miles from the bog where he died 2,000 years ago.

Man had been strangled. The lack of clothing and absence of any sign of struggle indicated that he had been a willing sacrificial victim. Further examination buttressed the theory and added one more clue to Tollund Man's fate: His last meal was a gruel of barley, linseed, and an assortment of weed seeds. These were the scant foodstuffs of the end of winter. Perhaps, scientists concluded, Tollund Man had offered himself in a springtime sacrifice entreating the gods to send plentiful crops.

Their investigations complete, scientists decided to maintain with their own chemicals the natural preservation process that was interrupted when the corpse was unearthed. Tollund Man's head—"the best-preserved human head to have survived from antiquity in any part of the world," according to one scholar—was subjected to a year-long process in which it was soaked in successive baths of formalin, acetic acid, alcohol, toluol, and kerosene, then steeped in warm wax. Although the procedure shrank the head by about one-eighth, the ancient visage remained perfect in features and proportions, and ready for display in the Silkeborg Museum of Central Jutland, located about six miles from Tollund Man's original resting place. □

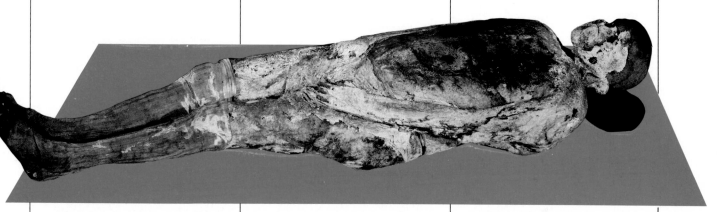

Clean Corpses

Ashes to ashes, dust to dust: That is, for most Westerners, the accepted course of the human body after death. But although a couple unearthed by road workers in 1875 may have lain beneath the soil of downtown Philadelphia for many decades, their bodies had become neither ash nor dust. Instead, they turned to soap, or something very much like it.

Although researchers do not agree on the date of the couple's burial—estimates range from the 1790s to sometime after 1824—they are certain what happened to the flesh once it was interred. Fatty tissues, bacteria, enzymes, and the unusually high alkaline content of the marshy grave site created a chemical reaction that turned both bodies into adipocere, a waxy substance akin to soap. Because soap does not deteriorate easily, the process, once complete, preserved their shapes almost perfectly.

But not pleasantly: The Soap Lady, as she is called, was described by a former curator of the Mutter Museum in Philadelphia as "one of the most revolting objects that can be imagined." Nevertheless, the Soap Lady can still be seen there. Her companion, the Soap Man, is owned, but no longer displayed, by the Smithsonian Institution's National Museum of Natural History in Washington, D.C. □

Alkalis and other chemicals in the soil beneath downtown Philadelphia, Pennsylvania, turned the body of a yellow fever victim into a soapy substance.

The first person to be cremated in the United States was Henry Laurens, a South Carolina planter and signer of the Treaty of Paris, which ended the American Revolution. He died on December 8, 1792, and was cremated the following day, according to his wishes.

Brain Trust

Canadian physician Sir William Osler was one of the most influential medical practitioners in the late nineteenth and early twentieth centuries, and his theories about the heart and circulatory system have withstood the test of time. Less well known—and considerably less successful—were the doctor's investigations of the brain, especially the connection between brain size and intelligence.

Osler followed cadavers into the autopsy room in order to measure and weigh their brains. He studied brains removed from executed murderers, hoping to find deformities that would explain their evil ways. And in 1889, Osler formed the American Anthropometric Society in Philadelphia. Now defunct, the society was truly a brain trust, whose members were among the most distinguished minds of the time. They included Osler himself, poet Walt Whitman, and pioneering dinosaur-bone hunter Edward Drinker Cope. Its president was Joseph Leidy, a prominent Philadelphia physician. Yet the most remarkable thing about the American Anthropometric Society was not the exclusive membership, but the price of admission: Every member had to pledge his brain to science—during his lifetime and thereafter.

Osler's own brain and those of a score of other society members were willed to the Wister Institute, a private medical research center at the University of Pennsylvania. Unfortunately, they never fulfilled the hopes of their original owners. Twentieth-century researchers regarded the brains as curiosities, not scientific assets, and in 1987 Philadelphia's Mutter Museum took possession of them. One brain did not make the move: Five years earlier, a clumsy laboratory worker had dropped Walt Whitman's gray matter, and it had to be discarded. □

Have a Heart

In 1822, four years after her eerie novel *Frankenstein* was published, Mary Shelley added a unique ornament to her desk—the heart of her drowned husband, Percy Bysshe Shelley. Rescued from the funeral pyre by a friend, Percy's charred and shriveled heart remained with Mary until her death in 1851.

Although preserving a cherished heart may seem macabre to modern tastes, at the time it was a romantic gesture in keeping with a centuries-old tradition. Some experts trace the practice of giving the heart special postmortem treatment to ancient embalming customs. But more modern versions seem to have started as a matter of convenience with the followers of the ascetic Robert D'Arbrissel in France. When he died in 1117, one monastery he had built, at Fontevrault, was honored with his body and another, at Orsan, with his heart.

When Richard the Lion-Hearted died in 1199 while warring in France, his body was buried at Fontevrault Abbey, but his heart went to Rouen's cathedral as a reward for the city's loyalty.

Some 500 years later, James II of England willed that his body be de-

Philadelphia's Mutter Museum displays both the brain and a portrait of Canadian physician Sir William Osler.

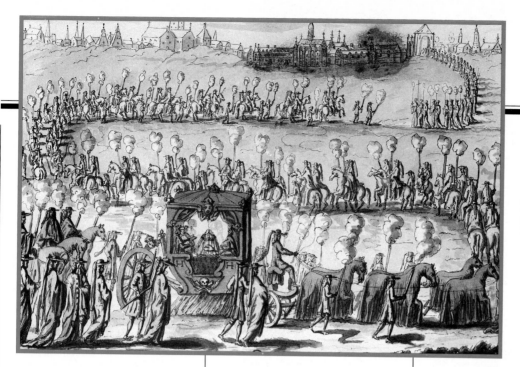

This seventeenth-century print shows the heart of France's King Henry IV being transported with royal honors to the Jesuit college of La Flèche in 1610.

livered to the English Benedictine church in Paris and later to Westminster Abbey. But his heart was his mother's: It was buried near hers at the Convent de la Visitation at Chaillot, which she founded.

More recently, following the death of British writer Thomas Hardy in 1928, his body was cremated, but his heart was buried in a bronze casket beside that of his wife under a yew tree at Stinsford in Dorset. His ashes were interred in Poet's Corner at Westminster Abbey.

Had Hardy's heart gone to Westminster Abbey, it would have been quite at home: At least fifty-four tiny grave slabs and diminutive effigies in the abbey purport to contain hearts of the great and famous. □

Second Career

For fifty years, John "Pop" Reed was a theater electrician, the man behind the lights in Philadelphia's famed Walnut Street Theater, the oldest continuously operated theater in America. He spent his days and nights contriving the lighting effects that would enhance some of America's greatest performances. All the while, however, Reed had a yen for a career in front of the footlights. Finally, he calculated a way to achieve his dream.

Before he died in 1891 at the age of eighty-three, Reed specified in his will that his head "be separated from my body, the latter to be buried in a grave; the former, duly prepared, to be brought to the theatre, where I served all my life, and to be employed to represent the skull of Yorick"—the object addressed by Shakespeare's anguished Hamlet during the graveyard soliloquy that begins, "Alas, poor Yorick."

The theater's management was happy to comply: Skulls were expensive props, and they were always in short supply. □

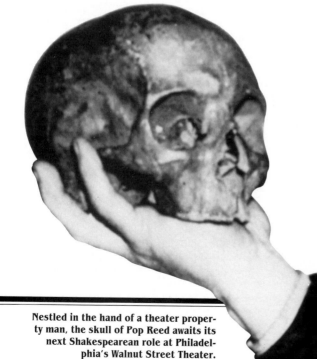

Nestled in the hand of a theater property man, the skull of Pop Reed awaits its next Shakespearean role at Philadelphia's Walnut Street Theater.

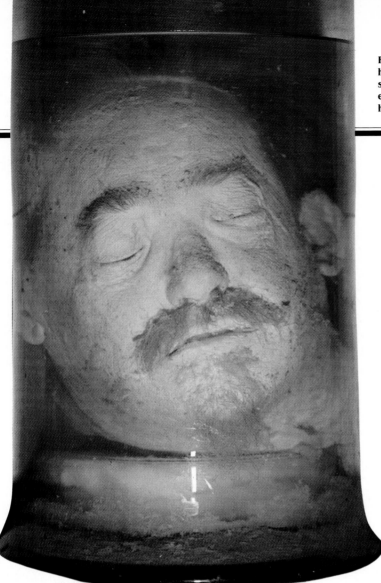

Preserved in beeswax, the head of phrenologist Cesare Lombroso joined others in his collection after his death in 1909.

Haydn Seek

The renowned Austrian composer Joseph Haydn enjoyed a long and brilliant career, three decades of it under the patronage of the noble Esterházy family. Haydn's works were performed in every European capital, and by the time he died in 1809 at the age of seventy-seven, Europe's culturati ranked Haydn's genius with that of his brilliant contemporary Mozart.

But one person viewed the music world's loss as a rare bit of good fortune. Three nights after its burial, Haydn's body was dug up and its head was removed by a team of graverobbers led by none other than Prince Nicholas Esterházy's own secretary, Joseph Carl Rosenbaum. This worthy was an amateur in the popular pseudoscience of phrenology. In the composer's passing, Rosenbaum saw a golden opportunity to correlate Haydn's eminent abilities with the bumps of his head. Accordingly, the secretary discarded Haydn's brain, had all of the flesh removed from the skull, and after due manipulation and study, pronounced "the bumps of music fully developed" on the great composer's cranium.

Its purpose fulfilled, the stolen skull was set to rest with others in Rosenbaum's collection. The theft went unnoticed for eleven years, until 1820, when the Esterházys exhumed the composer's body for reburial in a grand mausoleum at the family's palace in Eisenstadt, where Haydn had served for many years. Rosenbaum was immediately suspected, but he denied any knowledge of the robbery. However, a crony, a local prison warden named Johann Nepomuk Peter, spilled the beans and implicated his friend. By

Class of the Head

Italy's Cesare Lombroso was an internationally known psychiatrist and criminologist in the late 1800s. He was also a phrenologist—a believer in the notion, quite popular in his day, that the bumps and hollows of a person's head reveal character and intelligence. Lombroso amassed phrenological data with the conviction that it could teach him to detect criminal tendencies in people. In the course of his study, Lombroso gathered a large and widely celebrated collection of human heads that he preserved whole in glass bottles in his laboratory.

Toward the end of the nineteenth century, however, phrenology fell into disfavor, and Lombroso's studies were no longer considered relevant to criminology. Moreover, public criticism of the professor's collection mounted because it consisted almost entirely of the heads of poor people and criminals.

Lombroso could not turn the tide of opinion, but he did make a lasting testament to his faith in phrenology. His will dictated that his head be removed, classified, measured, and preserved in beeswax beside the others in his collection. □

that time Rosenbaum was a former Esterházy employee—he had been sacked by Prince Nicholas over a love affair that displeased the prince—and he could avoid jail only by handing over a head. When he dipped into his collection, however, Rosenbaum came up with another skull, not Haydn's.

The real item was much handled. At first it stayed in the former secretary's collection, but on his death in 1829, it was bequeathed to Peter, the warden. On his demise in 1838, Peter's widow gave the skull to her physician, Carl Haller, a professor of medicine in Vienna. In 1852, it passed to pathologist Carl Rokitansky, who hoped to house it in a museum he was planning. The archive was never built, however, and after Rokitansky's death his sons donat-ed Haydn's cranium to Vienna's Society of the Friends of Music. In 1895, the society enshrined the great composer's skull in a glass case, where it lay for more than half a century. Finally, in 1954, after long negotiations between the society, the city of Vienna, and the Austrian province of Burgenland of which Eisenstadt is the capital, skull and body were at last reunited in a marble tomb in Eisenstadt's baroque hilltop church, the Bergkirche. □

A heart pacemaker may keep on ticking long after its host has ceased kicking. Pacemaker batteries can last up to eight years. But the law requires that nuclear-powered pacemakers be removed before a person is buried.

The bishop of Burgenland blesses Joseph Haydn's skull during the ceremony reuniting it with remains of the composer's body at Eisenstadt, Austria, in 1954.

Family Tree

Roger Williams, the founder of Rhode Island, was buried like many of his seventeenth-century contemporaries in his own backyard. After his interment in 1683, other graves joined his, and trees grew up and shaded the plot. One in particular, a spreading, gnarled apple tree, seemed to embrace the souls beneath its branches. According to Williams's descendants, appearances above ground reflected activity below. The tree, they said, had devoured Williams's body.

In 1860, the family decided to move its illustrious ancestor to a more suitable tomb. The grave, however, yielded no human remains at all—only some rusty nails and a large, intrusive tree root could be found where Roger Williams's body should have been.

The apple tree root, the family contended, had grown into the coffin and absorbed Williams's unembalmed body as a rich source of nutrients. More imaginative members of the clan insisted that the root even had a human shape. And, in fact, the structure does have a thick torso segment that branches into two "legs" *(left)*. Some viewers have perceived the contours of knees, ankles, feet, and toes along its lower stretches. A second root found in the coffin resembles, to some, an arm and a hand.

Counting Roger Williams as absent from his grave, the family declined to rebury the ravenous larger root. Instead, they presented it to the Rhode Island Historical Society in Providence, where its shape still beguiles visitors. □

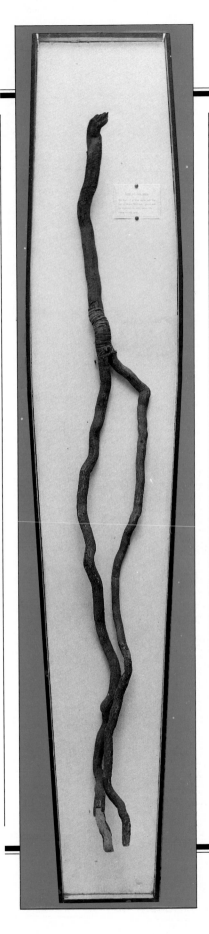

Pointed Memory

Despite his contributions to learning, the controversial astronomer Galileo Galilei merited only minimal honors when he died in 1642. Rather than allowing his body to lie within the main church of Florence's Santa Croce, Church authorities had him buried beneath the floor of Santa Croce's bell tower, near the chapel of Saints Cosmas and Damian. Nearly a century after this, in 1737, Galileo's full eminence was finally recognized, and his corpse was transferred to a mausoleum within the nearby Church of Santa Croce.

But the move was costly to the corpse. One overzealous Galileo admirer, Anton Francesco Cori, stole the middle finger of the astronomer's right hand. Other enthusiasts removed two more fingers, a rib, and several teeth.

The teeth and two fingers disappeared. But the rib still reposes in a case at the University of Padua. And, in an urn resting on an alabaster pedestal in Florence's Museum of the History of Science, Galileo's middle finger remains enshrined *(above)*, pointing toward the heavens that he once mapped. □

Missing Parts

In the four years of America's bitter Civil War, nearly half a million soldiers and sailors were treated for battle injuries. As many as four-fifths of the wounded lived, but the primitive medicine practiced during the mid-nineteenth century extracted a gruesome toll from many of them: the loss of a limb. Baskets filled with amputated arms and legs were piled outside the rough operating theaters of military hospitals, confirming the anguish within.

Most of this grisly harvest was silently buried, unmarked and forgotten, in battlefield graveyards. But not all. When Confederate General Stonewall Jackson lost his left arm to the surgeon's saw after the Battle of Chancellorsville in Virginia, a chaplain buried it

in a nearby cornfield, where today it is marked by an inscribed stone.

Similarly, a black metal plaque at the Navy Yard in Washington, D.C., marks the burial site of the amputated leg of Union Army Colonel Ulric Dahlgren, who lost his limb as a twenty-year-old officer skirmishing in the streets of Hagerstown, Maryland. A Marine honor guard escorted the leg to the Navy Yard, placed it in a box draped with the Stars and Stripes, and sealed it in the cornerstone of the post's foundry.

Perhaps the most bizarre fate to befall a missing limb involved the amputated leg of Union General Daniel Sickles. During the Battle of Gettysburg, a Confederate cannonball shattered Sickles's right leg. A circular directing field doctors to send to the office of the surgeon general "specimens of morbid anatomy, surgical or medical," prompted the general to have his leg packed in a miniature coffin and delivered to the Army Medical Museum in Washington. It was accompanied by the general's card, which read "Compliments of Gen. D.E.S."

Sickles was a wildly passionate and flamboyant man. He had been a congressman before the war and had used the then-novel defense of temporary insanity to escape conviction for murdering Philip Barton Key, the son of patriot Francis Scott Key. Philip had been conducting an affair with Sickles's wife. Given the general's temperament, no one was surprised after the war when he began observing the anniversary of Gettysburg by taking friends to view his leg. Remains of the limb still rest in a glass case near a lock of Lincoln's hair and other historic artifacts in what is now called the National Museum of Health and Medicine in Washington. □

Union General Daniel "Peg Leg" Sickles grasps the handle of his sword and strikes a heroic pose at a military ceremony.

One company's high-flying promise to its clients was an eternity in orbit in a golden capsule such as this one.

Death on the Wing

Although he was listed in the New York telephone directory as an undertaker, Dick Falk thought of himself as something else. "Actually," Falk once declared, "I'm an overtaker. I don't take people down, I take them up."

That was only half the truth, however, because in the end, Dick Falk let all of his customers down. Falk was one of several enterprising and flamboyant entrepreneurs whose businesses have been dedicated to scattering the ashes of their deceased clients near and far.

Once the pilot for his airborne enterprise, Falk, who was seventy-nine in 1991, eventually gave up the controls—but not his active participation. Sporting a snow white goatee and a mustache like that of the late artist Salvador Dali—for whom he was once a press agent—he still cut a dashing figure as he rode as a passenger in a small rented plane, scattering ashes from an oatmeal box. Drop sites were, of course, determined by the client. For instance, one man, who had spent much of his life as an inmate of New York's

Sing Sing Prison, asked that his remains be dropped over the penitentiary. Falk himself, long a lover of show business, planned to be dispersed over New York City's Times Square.

Oatmeal boxes were not the style for high-tech overtaker Terry Haglund of Minneapolis, Minnesota, who launched a service called Aerial Burials in 1977. Haglund loaded his clients' ashes into a thirty-inch-long device called an Aerial Dispersal Tube that was fastened to his aircraft's wing. A tug on a cord caused the tube to release the remains precisely on target. For one Haglund client, the objective was a bar where he had spent a great deal of his time. Another asked to have the ashes of his detested mother-in-law dropped exactly halfway around the world from his home.

Clients who liked Terry Haglund's service would probably have loved a company called Celestis, started in the early 1980s by two retirees—an aerospace engineer and a cemetery executive. Celestis was strategically based in Melbourne, Florida, not far from NASA's space center at Cape Canaveral. Customers with the right

stuff—about $3,900, or the price of a round-trip ticket on the Concorde at the time—could sign up with the firm to have their ashes packed in a lipstick-size canister and launched 1,900 miles into orbit in a gold-plated capsule. There, as the sun glinted off the shiny surface, the departed were to remain always visible to their earthbound loved ones—at least, to loved ones with telescopes. Unfortunately, Celestis went out of business in 1988 before orbiting a single customer. □

Terry Haglund displays the Aerial Dispersal Tube used by his unusual firm, Aerial Burials.

Bier Barrel

In twenty-four years of life, Nancy Adams Martin accomplished little of particular note. But in death both her body and her reputation were memorably preserved.

Nance, as she was called, was one of five children of clipper ship captain Silas H. Martin and his wife. In May of 1857, Nance and her brother John embarked with their father on what must have been a seafaring family's version of the Grand Tour, a yearlong voyage aboard Silas's ship, the *Martin Clipper.* The ship departed from her home port of Wilmington, North Carolina, heading for the Caribbean and its exotic ports of call. It was a star-crossed venture because before long Nancy fell seriously ill. Too far from home to return and still far from a port and medical assistance, the worried father pressed onward.

Nancy soon died. Concern became grief, accompanied by the need to make an agonizing choice. The captain had contracts to fulfill, and turning back to Wilmington could destroy his livelihood and his family's future. But he could not bear to see his daughter's body consigned to the waves. Father and son agreed that the voyage must continue, but they also found an alternative to burial at sea. Like all sailing ships of the time, the *Martin Clipper* was well stocked with wine and spirits for the crew. The Martins determined that Nancy's body could be preserved for interment at home if they put it inside a large cask filled with alcohol from the ship's ration. To keep the remains from floating and jostling inside the cask, the sorrowing pair tied Nance's body to a chair and nailed it in place. Whiskey, rum, and wine followed the deceased into the cask. The barrel then was sealed and stowed in a cabin belowdecks.

Unfortunately, Captain Martin's sorrows did not end with his daughter's death. Four months after she died, young John Martin was swept overboard in a midnight squall. He was never found, and the twice-bereaved father at last turned his vessel homeward.

Back in Wilmington, the family decided not to remove Nance's body from its cask, reasoning that spirits were probably better than soil for preserving the body. At the funeral, grieving friends and relatives gathered at the graveside in Oakdale Cemetery as the enormous barrel, still topped off with liquor, was lowered into its grave. □

Pyramid Scheme

Not only does its pledge of eternal preservation necessarily exclude a money-back guarantee, but Salt Lake City's Summum Company cheerfully promises to soak its customers. The soaking is a literal one—a month in a vat of wine and herbs. Summum—whose Latin name describes the greatest, the highest, or the most extreme—provides a way for the modern-day deceased to head for the afterlife in a manner befitting a nobleman of ancient Egypt.

For the price of a conventional funeral—a princely one—the firm will mummify its customers and package them for posterity like the royalty of old. The process begins by soaking the deceased for thirty days in a steel vat of chemical preservatives, herbs, and wine. The wine is white; red discolors the skin. Ordinarily, a domestic house blend—which Summum also sells to churches as a sacramental wine—is used.

Once well steeped, the body is treated with oils and lotions to keep the skin smooth and supple for years to come. Then the corpse is wrapped in gauze made impervious to the grave's depredations with coatings of fiberglass, polyethyl- ◊

ene, and plaster. The encapsulated remains are injected with inert gas, providing a final tier of protection against the ravages of time and the atmosphere. Except for the use of modern materials, the process follows that used by the embalmers of the pharaohs.

In its royal treatment of modern clients, Summum offers a range of sarcophagi that it calls "mummi-forms." At the low end is a durable and practical fiberglass enclosure. Grander models are made of stain-less steel and bronze, and all are available with such decorations as gold headdresses, jeweled inlays, carved phoenixes, and golden scarabs. By the time the client's life mask is sculpted on the mummi-form's face, the tab for emulating Egyptian king Tuthankhamen can exceed $100,000. □

Once encased in plaster and plastic *(below, right)*, a Summum client can be treated like Egyptian royalty *(left)*—for a princely sum.

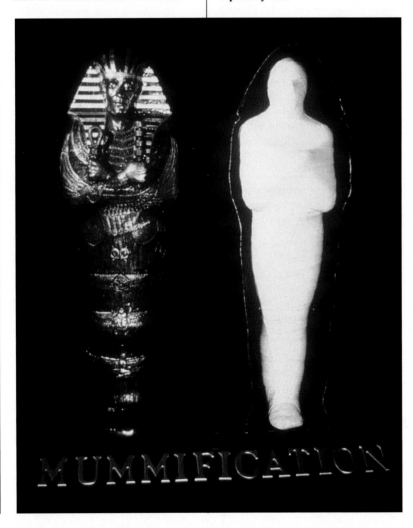

Upsetting decorum as well as furniture,
an indomitable Hannah Dagoe lands a
punch on her would-be executioner in a
contemporary engraving.

Cheating the Hangman

In the 1700s, a London court sentenced Hannah Dagoe to hang for looting a poor widow's apartment of all her worldly goods. But Dagoe had other ideas about her fate.

Dagoe, described as "a strong masculine woman" in her midthirties, paid no heed to the priest who rode to the Tyburn gallows with her, supposedly to hear her last prayers, on May 4, 1763. When the cart arrived at the place of execution, Dagoe worked loose of the ropes that bound her, fended off the executioner with a sturdy punch, and began to strip, throwing her hat, cloak, and other articles of clothing to the cheering crowd.

Her unruly act greatly annoyed the executioner, since the belongings of the condemned were rightfully his. He managed to wriggle the noose around Dagoe's neck, only to have her cheat him out of a hanging: Defiant to the end, she flung herself out of the cart, breaking her neck and dying at once. □

SAN FRANCISCO firemen struggle feverishly to free John Reid, whose hands protrude from a vat of barley in which he suffocated. Reid, a student working a summer job in 1952 at a San Francisco brewery, was alone when he slipped into the vat as it was being emptied.

Balthasar's Reward

The shabby newcomer to William of Orange's court at Delft in the Netherlands in 1584 introduced himself as François Guyon. He was, he said, a poor orphan and a Protestant, like the prince and his followers. William was moved to sympathy when he heard that Guyon had no decent shoes, and he ordered that the young man be given twelve crowns to buy a new pair.

But Guyon had wormed his way into the Dutch court under false colors, and he had other plans for the money. His real name was Balthasar Gerardt, and he was a devoted follower of Spain's Catholic king Philip II, whose hold on much of the Netherlands had been broken by Prince William. In 1580, in the midst of his long and bitter struggle with the Protestant prince, Philip had called for his opponent's death with a promise of 25,000 ducats to the successful assassin. Gerardt had vowed to answer his call, and with the prince's twelve crowns he now bought, instead of a pair of shoes, a pair of small pistols with which to slay his benefactor.

Several months before his arrival at

Obscure in death as well as life, Balthasar Gerardt's visage is known only by this Dutch painting from the seventeenth century.

Delft, Gerardt had made an unsuccessful appeal to Philip's ally, the prince of Parma, for an advance on assassination expenses. Parma had already financed a number of would-be assassins with no success. Besides, he was unimpressed with the latest applicant. "The character of the person did not promise well for an enterprise of so great importance," he later wrote to Philip.

Parma had misjudged his supplicant. On July 10, 1584, Gerardt ambushed the fifty-one-year-old

William as he left a family lunch, shooting him in the chest. Quickly captured, the assassin confessed proudly and boasted of his guilt.

A series of gruesome punishments was meted out to the unrepentant Gerardt in Delft's marketplace. The hand that had held the fatal firearm was burned, and other parts of Gerardt's body were roasted until the flesh could be removed with tongs. He was quartered and disemboweled, and his heart was cut out and thrown into his lifeless face. As a final indignity, his severed head was displayed on a stake.

Arguing that too much time had elapsed since he had made the offer, King Philip balked at paying the promised reward to Balthasar Gerardt's survivors. However, with some prodding from the prince of Parma, the king came up with a substitute for the 25,000 ducats. He granted the family three small estates confiscated from William years before and threw in a patent of nobility as well.

Catholic Europe hailed Balthasar Gerardt as a martyr, but he accomplished nothing for Spain. In fact, William's sons brought still more territory into the Protestant fold and eventually established the Dutch Republic. □

Loyal Servant

Mary, Queen of Scots, condemned for treason by her cousin Queen Elizabeth I, walked to her execution on February 8, 1587. At the time, all thought she walked alone. But in fact, a hidden companion took the dreadful last steps with her.

After the queen had said her last prayer and the ax had fallen on her slender neck, the executioner start-ed: Mary's skirts suddenly moved. As witnesses gaped, out from beneath the queen's dark red pet-ticoat crept her little lap dog, a Skye terrier.

"He took up a position between the body and the head, which he kept until some one came and re-moved him, and this had to be done by violence," a later biogra-pher reported.

The terrier was washed and washed again in order to rid him of the blood that had soaked his wiry coat; Queen Elizabeth was afraid that anything touched by the Scot-tish queen's blood would be wor-shiped as a relic.

Although servants tried to tempt the little dog to eat after the execu-tion, he refused to take a mouthful. His mourning for the star-crossed queen never ceased, and he soon followed her into untimely death. □

The Unquiet Countess

Margaret Pole, countess of Salisbury, and her family learned to their sorrow what vengeance their king and cousin, Henry VIII of England, was capable of. Henry had reason to be uneasy about the Poles. Scions of the York clan, they had a hereditary claim to the throne equal to that of Henry's Tudor clan. Nevertheless, the Yorks and the Tudors had numerous ties. Henry handed over his little daughter Mary to Mar-

garet Pole's care, and Henry paid for her son Reginald's education at Oxford University and in Italy.

In 1532, Henry created an irreparable schism between himself and the Poles. In order to divorce his wife, Catherine of Aragon, Henry left the Roman Catholic church, but the Poles vehemently declined to follow him. Henry was not churchless for long. The Church of England was formed at his behest, and he

declared himself to be its sovereign.

Taking violent exception to the king's actions, Reginald Pole penned a lengthy condemnation and sent it to the king in 1536.

As if the scathing treatise were not enough, Pole, now a cardinal, went on two diplomatic missions for the pope to unite Europe's Catholic monarchs against the English king. Henry, livid at his cousin's treachery, vowed he would wipe out the Poles. His first victim was Lord Montague, Margaret's eldest son,

Margaret Pole, painted by a contemporary artist in more placid times *(above)*, led her executioner on a grisly chase *(right)*, to the horror of the witnesses.

who was executed on trumped-up charges of treason.

Age was no shield for sixty-five-year-old Margaret Pole. Accused by the king of having once planned to marry Reginald to Princess Mary, who had remained a Catholic, Margaret was hauled off to the Tower of London in 1539. She staunchly resisted her bullying interrogators, one of whom sighed that she was "rather a strong and constant man than a woman."

Margaret Pole was never released from the Tower, where she spent two miserable years. On the morning of May 27, 1541, she was awakened and given dreadful news: The king had ordered her to be executed that morning. Margaret was taken to a remote courtyard. Asking everyone present to pray for her soul and for the king's, she sent Princess Mary her love and the message: "Blessed are they who suffer persecution for justice' sake."

Margaret made the task of the inexperienced stand-in for the regular executioner as difficult as possible. She refused to lay her head on the executioner's block—it was for traitors, she said, and "I am none." According to most accounts, Margaret ran around the courtyard with her executioner in pursuit. Her end was an especially brutal affair. The executioner "hacked her head and shoulders almost to pieces," an eyewitness reported.

The Poles' power did not die with Margaret. When Princess Mary assumed her father's crown in 1553, Pope Julius III appointed Reginald Pole his legate in England, and Mary became extremely reliant on his advice. It was the closest any Pole came to sitting on the throne—but close enough to give the family the last laugh on Henry. □

Kindly Victim

President William McKinley was a popular man, and he had no reason to expect anything but warm greetings as he stood in the receiving line at the Pan-American Exposition in Buffalo, New York, on the afternoon of September 6, 1901.

Nor was he alarmed when a thin young man by the name of Leon Czolgosz reached out with a hand bandaged in a handkerchief. McKinley reached out, too, expecting a handshake. Instead, he was struck by two shots from a pistol concealed under the man's bandage.

Security guards wrestled the assassin to the ground and began beating him with rifles and clubs. The wounded McKinley watched with a look of wonder and reproach as a Secret Service man dragged Czolgosz to his feet and slugged him on his already-bloody jaw. Scanning his assailant's battered face, the president murmured to his guards not to hurt the "poor misguided fellow."

Willaim McKinley died on September 14. The kind words of the president are credited with saving Czolgosz's life—if only briefly. An avowed anarchist, he was tried and sentenced to die in the electric chair. At his execution on October 29, almost two months after his crime, the twenty-eight-year-old Czolgosz said only: "I am not sorry. I did this for the working people. My only regret is that I haven't been able to see my father." □

Dramatic Demise

King Gustavus III of Sweden unwittingly set the stage for his own demise, and had he not been the evening's victim he would doubtless have enjoyed the drama of the occasion. Crowned in 1771, Gustavus was a gifted ruler and, by late-eighteenth-century standards, an enlightened one. But his real passion was for the arts. He encouraged a neoclassical style of architecture now called Gustavian, and he founded the Swedish Academy, the royal opera, the royal ballet, and a theater. The king loved drama best of all. He wrote and produced numerous plays in French, the language of the cultured at the time.

Gustavus was, paradoxically, an autocratic reformer. He granted peasants the right to own land, even though the move angered many Swedish aristocrats. But the rich and the poor were in agreement on one point: They resented the king's extravagant spending on plays and masked balls.

One especially outraged landowner, Jacob Johan Anckarström, determined that Gustavus must die and that he himself would kill the king. On March 16, 1792, a masked ball was held at the royal opera. While the king was dining there in his private chambers, he received a letter warning him of an assassination attempt. Unruffled, he finished his dinner and strolled to his private box overlooking the ballroom. Gustavus stood watching the revelers for about fifteen minutes, then remarked, "If anyone had wanted to kill me, that would have been their best possible chance."

Then the king descended into the merry crowd below, clearly identified by one adornment on the breast of his costume: the medal of the Order of the Seraphim. Only those of very high rank held that medal. As partygoers swirled around the floor, Anckarström drew a pistol from his black domino cloak and felled the monarch with one shot in the back.

The orchestra's quadrille obscured the sound of the shot, but a few of the revelers heard Gustavus cry *"Je suis blessé!"* (I am wounded!) and saw him stagger. The king was quickly led away to his private rooms. Guards locked the doors of the opera house and began questioning the guests. Authorities found the pistol, which Anckarström had tossed aside in the ballroom. Anckarström was arrested the following day and was later beheaded. The king survived for two weeks before dying of blood poisoning at the age of forty-six. More than sixty years later, King Gustavus's end was immortalized in Guiseppe Verdi's opera *Un Ballo in Maschera* (A Masked Ball). □

A contemporary German chronicler captured the faces of stunned merrymakers who witnessed the 1792 assassination of Sweden's King Gustavus III *(right center of engraving)*.

No Lifesaver

American poet Hart Crane was fond of using the sea as a metaphor for life and death. "The bottom of the sea is cruel," he once wrote. On April 27, 1932, the talented but darkly tormented Crane made the ultimate leap from symbol to reality. He flung himself from the stern of an ocean liner into the Caribbean Sea, committing suicide at the age of thirty-two.

Crane's life had been a chronicle of instability and despair. Nevertheless, he had managed to write a number of highly acclaimed works including *The Bridge,* a poem cycle that uses the Brooklyn Bridge as a metaphor for connecting the past and the present.

After these early successes, Crane went to Mexico in 1931 with the aim of writing an epic poem along the lines of *The Bridge.* He failed to produce it and instead spent a year drinking and brawling. "He was possessed by a demon that gave him no peace," Peggy Cowley, his fiancée, wrote.

April of 1932 found Crane and Cowley sailing back to the United States aboard the liner *Orizaba.* The poet was in despair over his artistic failures, his lack of money, and his inability to come to terms with his bisexuality. His last night seemed to summarize all his difficulties. The *Orizaba* sailed from Havana, and soon Crane had drunk so much and caused such a commotion that the purser consigned Crane to his cabin and nailed the door shut. Crane managed to escape. Reappearing on deck around 3:30 a.m., he climbed onto the ship's rail but was wrestled down by the night watchman and returned to his cabin. In the morning, a shaky Crane said to Cowley, "I'm not going to make it, dear. I'm utterly disgraced." Cowley was in her cabin brushing her hair just before noon when the boat suddenly stopped. "Hart," Cowley screamed and ran onto the deck.

Lifeboats were already being lowered into the water.

Crane had come out onto the deck in pajamas and overcoat, thrown the coat off, and leaped into the sea. His body was never found.

Ironically, Crane's father, a successful Cleveland businessman, had been the inventor of Life Savers candies, whose wrapper featured a sailor tossing a life preserver. □

Poet Hart Crane poses before the subject of one of his major poetic works, New York's Brooklyn Bridge.

Self-Sentenced

Pennsylvania state treasurer R. Budd Dwyer's world was disintegrating. He had been accused, tried, and convicted of conspiracy, mail fraud, perjury, and racketeering for taking a $300,000 kickback on a state computer contract, and on January 23, 1987, a judge would pronounce his sentence. Dwyer knew that he might be sent to jail for as many as fifty-five years.

On the day before his sentencing, Dwyer called a press conference. When he entered his office to face the assembled reporters and television crews, the treasurer ordered that the door to his secretaries' office be shut. He also dismissed most of his aides, instructing only a few men to remain. Near tears, Dwyer distributed a press statement twenty pages long and attacked the people he considered responsible for his downfall, including former governor Richard Thornburgh, the press, the FBI, the prosecutor, the judge who tried him, and the jury that convicted him. He called himself "a modern Job," alluding to the biblical character who had suffered one terrible burden after another.

The disintegration was nearly complete. Dwyer handed three envelopes to his aides, then pulled a .357 magnum revolver from his briefcase. "Please leave the room," Dwyer said, "as this will . . . as this will hurt someone." Then, as television cameras rolled and horrified reporters and members of his staff cried out, Dwyer put the gun barrel in his mouth, clamped his lips around it, and pulled the trigger. Dying instantly, Dwyer lay slumped against a cabinet, blood running from his mouth and nose.

Dwyer had planned the details of his death carefully. The tables and chairs in his office had been arranged so that no one could reach him quickly enough to prevent him from pulling the trigger. Dwyer had withheld the twenty-first and last page of his press statement, preferring for it to be read after he was dead. It revealed his resolve not to resign. Quoting from *The Shame of the Cities*, by turn-of-the-century muckraker Lincoln Steffens, Dwyer said he would die in office to "see if the shameful facts, spread out in all their shame, will not burn through our civic shamelessness and set fire to American pride." However, the statement contained no new information that exonerated Dwyer.

The envelopes Dwyer had given to his aides just before he died contained instructions for his funeral, his organ-donor card, and a letter asking Governor Robert Casey to appoint Dwyer's wife as the new treasurer. When Casey learned of Dwyer's request, he said the appointment was out of the question.

Like many other public officials found guilty of misdeeds, Dwyer blamed the press for many of his difficulties. His final document included a message for the media that was laden with mocking irony. "Last May I told you that after the trial, I would give you the story of the decade," he wrote. He may have done so, but there was no joy among the reporters. □

Card Bomb

William Kogut *(below)*, a thirty-six-year-old Polish lumberjack, sat morosely in San Quentin State Prison in the fall of 1930, awaiting execution for the murder of a woman of dubious virtue who ran an Oroville, California, rooming house near Kogut's lumber camp.

The murder that had taken place in May was routinely sordid. Mayme Guthrie sold drinks and probably provided services of a carnal nature at her rooming house. On the afternoon of her death, Guthrie served Kogut numerous glasses of bootleg liquor. Sometime during his drinking bout, Kogut took out a one-dollar pocket knife and cut the woman's throat. He never revealed why. "Only she and I know why I did it," he said. Motive hardly mattered to judge and jury, and Kogut was found guilty and sentenced to death.

Kogut did

agree that he deserved to die for his crime. However, he did not think that the state should punish him—he preferred to handle the job himself by committing suicide. "I make the law myself, a life for a life," Kogut told police after his arrest. "I kill someone, I should take my life right now." Jail authorities thought otherwise and took away anything he could use to hang himself.

The precaution foiled any suicide plans Kogut might have had during his trial. But suicidal thoughts remained with him after sentencing, when he was sent to San Quentin to await the gallows. Kogut then scrutinized his new surroundings for their suicidal possibilities.

Within four months, he had worked out a way to escape the executioner—a homemade pipe bomb. For a casing, Kogut

wrenched one of the hollow steel legs from his cot. Next, he tore several decks of playing cards into tiny pieces and jammed them into the steel leg. He plugged one of its ends tightly with a broom handle, then poured water in through the other to soak the torn-up cards.

Sometime early on October 20, Kogut laid the pipe bomb atop a small kerosene heater beside his cot. He then lay down and placed the bomb's open end against the top of his head.

Near dawn, the quiet of the prison was abruptly shattered. The heater had turned the water in the cot leg to steam. The pressure inside built up until the steam suddenly exploded out through the open end. The bits of playing cards were propelled out so forcefully that they penetrated Kogut's skull.

The methodical Kogut had composed a note for the warden to read after his death. "Do not blame my death on any one because I fixed everything myself. I never give up as long as I am living and have a chance, but this is the end." □

Snowball in Hell

Carl Hulsey was determined to turn his white billy goat Snowball *(left)* into a watchdog, whether Snowball wanted to be one or not. To that end, seventy-seven-year-old Hulsey, a retired poultry worker from Canton, Georgia, took to beating Snowball with a stick to make him more aggressive.

"Pa, this goat's going to kill you if you keep that up," Alma Hulsey warned her husband. She was right. On May 16, 1991, Hulsey once again approached the goat brandishing his stick. But this time Snowball landed the first blow. The 110-pound goat attacked his tormentor, butting Hulsey in the stomach and knocking him down. Hulsey ran for the porch. The goat bounded up the steps and butted him over the edge. Hulsey fell to the ground three feet below and died where he landed.

Although Mrs. Hulsey managed to chain Snowball to a post, he remained in a fighting mood. It took three men to wrestle him into the animal warden's truck. Snowball's anger seemed to infect several other Hulsey goats. Three climbed atop a sheriff's patrol car and began butting its blue flasher lights. They were not taken into custody.

For Snowball, the episode had a bittersweet ending. Although Hulsey's widow did not blame Snowball for her husband's death, she did say that she would be happy when the goat's meat was in her freezer.

Animal rights activists came to Snowball's defense, and hundreds of people called Cherokee County officials with adoption offers. In the end, Snowball was transferred to Noah's Ark, a shelter for abused and neglected animals south of Atlanta, where he was neutered—and rechristened Snow. □

Lawrence Oates's last agonizing steps
were depicted in this painting by J. G.
Dollman. It was completed in 1913, a
year after Oates's death.

Walk into Oblivion

During the antarctic summer of 1911-1912, explorers competed for the honor of being the first to reach the South Pole. Robert Falcon Scott's British team arrived on January 18—thirty-four days behind a group of Norwegians. Scott and his companions, Lawrence Oates, Edward Adrian Wilson, and H. R. Bowers, made their polar stay a short one—the trek from the British base camp on Ross Island had taken two months, and they wanted to beat the return of extreme cold weather.

But it struck soon and with a vengeance. The team had hardly begun its trip back when temperatures plunged, regularly reaching forty degrees below zero Fahrenheit. The going was very slow: The terrain was rough and broken, and the party was hauling heavy sledges loaded with equipment. The men husbanded their dwindling store of food and fuel carefully. An evening meal Scott described in his diary consisted of one cup of cocoa and a frozen piece of pemmican each.

In the unrelenting polar cold, Captain Oates's feet became so badly frostbitten that walking became a torture. "Poor Oates is unable to pull, sits on the sledge when we are track-searching—he is wonderfully plucky as his feet must be giving him great pain," Scott wrote on March 6, 1912. "If we were all fit I should have hopes of getting through, but the poor Soldier has become a terrible hindrance."

Oates's feet became gangrenous, and it took him two agonizing hours to put his boots on each morning. Still, he staggered on into the fierce winds until March 15, when he said he could go no farther. His mates were growing weaker by the day, and Oates urged them to leave him behind. He knew—they all knew—that he was slowing them down and dimming the already faint possibility that they would reach their next food cache, thirty miles away.

The men had already discussed what course to follow in such dreadful circumstances. Suicide was one option—the sacrifice of one in the interest of the rest. Under orders from Scott, each man carried a lethal dose of thirty opium tablets for just such an eventuality.

When Oates collapsed, however, his companions could not bear to leave him alone to a self-inflicted fate. Instead, they made camp for the night. Scott later speculated that Oates hoped he would not wake in the morning, thus relieving his companions of their burden.

But Oates survived the night, waking with the other men to a blizzard. Scott recorded Oates's last words to his friends: "He said, 'I am just going outside and I may be some time,' " wrote Scott. "He went out into the blizzard and we have not seen him since."

Scott, Wilson, and Bowers continued to slog on, but a heavy snowfall stalled them eleven miles from the food cache. All three of them died sometime around March 29, 1912. Their bodies, and Scott's heartbreaking diary, were recovered by later explorers, but Oates's body was never found. □

Fatal Joy

In late November of 1521, Pope Leo X was hunting at his villa at Magliana when he received welcome news: The troops of the Holy Roman Emperor, Charles V, had driven the French army from the northern Italian cities of Milan, Parma, and Piacenza. Leo, a member of Florence's wealthy and powerful Medici family, had supported Charles's efforts to expel the French from Italy.

The victories so overjoyed the pope that he ordered a huge, celebratory bonfire to be lit in his courtyard. He leaned out a window to observe the roaring fire, ignoring the damp and bitter north wind that whipped around his ears.

Upon his return to Rome, the pope asked his master of ceremonies about the propriety of a public observance to mark the Holy Roman Emperor's victory. It was not customary, the master of ceremonies explained, to rejoice over the outcome of a battle that had been waged between two Christian nations. If, however, the pope deemed the outcome an advantage to the Church, then a public celebration was perfectly proper.

Leo decided in favor of a celebration, but it never took place. The excitement and the weather proved too much for the pope, who had never had a strong constitution, and he fell ill. His physicians dismissed the sickness as a mere cold, but on December 1, just one week after the bonfire of victory, Leo X suddenly died.

Although poisoning was first suspected—or perhaps the judgment of an angry God for his taking sides in a Christian conflict—the forty-five-year-old pope, weakened by his respiratory ailment, most probably died of chronic malaria, which was endemic in Italy at the time. □

Jawboning

"God forbid that the right of speech be taken from us," U.S. senator Theodore G. Bilbo of Mississippi intoned piously during one of his interminable Senate speeches. And indeed, the right of speech was one that Bilbo used freely—and, some say, abused wantonly.

Theodore Bilbo was an old-style Southern Democrat; verbosity and vitriol were his stock in trade. He ground Latin, the Bible, and down-home slang into an artful amalgam that was occasionally eloquent and never concise.

"Friends, fellow citizens, brethren and sisters, hallelujah!" Bilbo began one campaign speech. "My opponents, yea, these unprincipled opponents who would convince you if they could that the man Bilbo is not a friend of the common man, the poor man, these opponents who have the dastardly, dew-lipped, brazen, sneering, pusillanimous, cold-blooded, insulting, lop-eared, blue-nosed, and un-Christian effrontery to ask you for your votes." That was only the preamble. The typical Bilbo speech could go on for hours. During one of his filibusters on the Senate floor, the gentleman from Mississippi spoke against proposed legislation for five days.

Bilbo was first elected to the U.S. Senate in 1934 after a long and scandal-tinged career in state politics, during which he served two terms as Mississippi's governor. After he won his seat, he promised his supporters that he would "make as much noise for the common people as Huey P. Long," the voluble senator from neighboring Louisiana.

In Washington, Bilbo flew the colors of racism and vehement segregation. In 1939, he proposed that the government ship all black people to Liberia. He repeatedly joined

filibusters against poll-tax reform bills that would enable blacks to vote. During Bilbo's 1946 reelection campaign, two Senate committees were investigating allegations that he had incited attacks against black voters and had received money and gifts from war contractors. Despite the probes, Bilbo won a third term in the Senate—and the chance to go on talking.

"It's my ancestors," the diminutive Bilbo once said to explain his logorrhea. "Half-French, where I get my loquacity and my gestures. The other half Irish, where I get my audacity. With that combination, a man can talk forever." It seemed that he might well do exactly that, but by the time he started his third term, cancer had already begun to eat away at his jaw. Three operations proved ineffective. Within a year of his reelection, on August 21, 1947, in New Orleans, the man who had made his reputation as the most long-winded member of a chamber of orators died—drugged and at long last speechless—at the age of sixty-nine. □

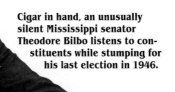

Cigar in hand, an unusually silent Mississippi senator Theodore Bilbo listens to constituents while stumping for his last election in 1946.

To Sleep, to Die

When Ying Yang went to bed on December 12, 1980, there was no reason to suspect that he would soon be dead. Yang, an apparently healthy twenty-seven-year-old Laotian immigrant living in Santa Ana, California, had passed the evening talking with his brother. Near dawn, Yang's wife awakened to hear him uttering odd gurgling noises. All of her attempts to rouse her husband from his deep sleep failed, and she summoned an ambulance. Nothing the medics tried helped Yang, and within two hours he was dead. The physicians who performed an autopsy on Yang discovered nothing to explain his unexpected demise.

It was a classic case of sudden unexplained death syndrome (SUDS), a bizarre disease that arrived in the United States during the 1970s and 1980s with Vietnamese and Laotian refugees such as Ying Yang who were fleeing war and its aftermath. SUDS is very choosy about its victims—they are overwhelmingly male, young, and seemingly healthy. And they are always Southeast Asian.

Why this group is so peculiarly vulnerable to SUDS, and why death should strike at night, presents medical experts with a knotty problem to solve. They do have some solid facts to go on. For one thing, SUDS is a well-known killer of young men in parts of Southeast Asia. Thus, the immigrants carried some vulnerability away with them when they left home. A second bit of evidence comes from autopsies. They reveal an anatomical abnormality that makes the victim's heart beat so wildly and erratically that ◊

he dies without warning. Researchers debate what causes the abnormality to develop in the first place and why it suddenly triggers the heart's lethal rhythms.

Physicians in Singapore have pointed an accusing finger at a bacterium that is common in Southeast Asian rice fields. Ninety percent of the Thai immigrants dying in Singapore of SUDS have been infected with the bacterium. Researchers wonder whether it lies dormant until some unknown factor rouses it to lethal activity.

Other scientists raise the possibility that a sleep disorder called a night terror is the villain. During such an episode, the sleeper endures overwhelming panic and a heartbeat that sometimes zooms to triple the normal rate in thirty seconds. Most people survive night terrors, but perhaps one of cataclysmic proportions is more than the heart can take. How the night terror phenomenon could become fatal among Southeast Asians alone is a mystery.

Since modern medicine has no way to protect them, many immigrants practice traditional methods of warding off SUDS. For some, that means disguising themselves as women—painting their fingernails red and donning women's clothing—to escape detection by the widow ghost, a spirit who goes in search of a husband and strikes dead the man she selects. □

The Force of Destiny

New York's Metropolitan Opera was sold out on the night of March 4, 1960. The evening marked the gala return to the Met of Italian diva Renata Tebaldi. This night she would sing Leonora in Giuseppe Verdi's grand opera *La Forza del Destino* (The Force of Destiny). Playing opposite her in the part of Don Carlo was the American baritone Leonard Warren, whose powerful voice and impressive girth endowed him with a grandeur that was equal to both Verdi and Tebaldi.

All eyes were riveted on Warren as he strode forward to sing his second-act aria, which began, *"Urna fatale del mio destino."* (Fatal urn of my destiny.) *"Morir!"* sang Don Carlo, pondering the injuries of Don Alvaro. *"Tremenda cosa!"*—"To die! A tremendous thing!"

This was Warren and Verdi at their melodramatic best; the audience's attention was fixed on the baritone as the last notes of his aria died and he began to sweep from the stage. The eyes widened. Mouths gaped. The huge man plunged face forward—like a falling column, said one colleague later. Leonard Warren lay motionless on the stage. The curtain fell, and the singer's wife, who had been in the audience, rushed backstage.

Half an hour later, the Metropolitan's general manager, Rudolf Bing, stepped before the curtain to inform the stunned audience that the performance had concluded. At the peak of his career, Leonard Warren had suffered a massive stroke during the fatal *Forza*, and all efforts to revive the singer had failed. □

In the role that marked his life and death, baritone Leonard Warren poses as Don Carlo for a 1943 issue of *Opera News.*

The Telltale Corpse

Rodrigo Borgia, a member of the family that schemed its way to power and wealth in the fifteenth century, used his appointment as cardinal and vice-chancellor of the Church to amass a tremendous fortune. He also fathered a number of children, including the infamous Lucrezia and her brother Cesare, on whom Niccolò Machiavelli modeled his political classic, *The Prince.*

Rodrigo's worldly ways were no obstacle to being elected pope in 1492. In fact, they may have done the trick, for it is widely supposed that he bribed his way into the position. Nor did Rodrigo change after becoming Pope Alexander VI. He is considered one of the most ambitious and corrupt of the worldly Renaissance popes.

Alexander VI died on August 18, 1503, after a two-week illness. He was seventy-three and enormously fat, wearing many of his life's excesses. In death, there was no papal majesty. His body swelled, darkened, and foamed at the mouth "like a kettle over the fire."

The extraordinary corruption of the pontiff's body led to rumors that he had been poisoned. Soon the story encompassed both the pope and his son Cesare. According to this story, both had been poisoned by their own hand, inadvertently drinking wine they had doctored to do away with an enemy cardinal. Cesare survived, the tale went, but not his father.

The rumor had the odor of justice about it, if not truth. "It was the will of the immortal gods," Cardinal Bembo wrote later, "that they who had killed with poison many princes of the Roman Republic, in order to obtain possession of their riches and treasures, should thus perish by their own act."

Modern science supplies an explanation for Alexander VI's death and his blackened body that is less titillating, if more plausible: that the pope died of malaria, a common ailment of the time, and the horrible state of his corpse was attributable to nothing more than the notorious August heat. □

His papal crown before him, Rodrigo Borgia—Pope Alexander VI—piously witnesses Christ's open tomb in a Vatican fresco by contemporary painter Pinturicchio.

Fatal Rhythm

As winter closed in on France in 1686, the nation fretted over the grave illness of King Louis XIV. But the monarch's condition reversed itself, and as he continued to improve steadily, celebration supplanted mourning.

The Sun King's return to health provided an occasion for Jean-Baptiste Lully *(above)*, the court composer, to discharge his chief responsibility—glorifying Louis whenever possible. Lully was an ambitious man. Although he was a native of Italy, the composer had managed to insinuate himself into the French court and now controlled opera performances throughout the country. Being named *secrétaire du roi* was a major coup for Lully, since the position was a privileged one usually reserved for an aristocrat. The Italian's exertions had made him both rich and famous.

In honor of the king's return to good health, Lully composed an anthem that was first performed on January 8, 1687. As a demonstration of his devotion to the king, Lully conducted the performance himself. Following the practice of the time, he marked the music's meter with a tall staff that he pounded loudly on the floor so that the singers and musicians could hear.

In the heat of the performance, Lully pounded his toe, raising a painful blister. It persisted and became infected, and Lully's physician, M. Alliot, advised him to have the toe amputated. Lully refused. Within days, gangrene had traveled through his foot and up his leg. Alliot told Lully that the limb must be amputated if he was to survive, but the musician would hear none of it. Suggesting a different sort of cure, Lully's acquaintance the duc de Vendôme called in a popular faith healer, the marquis de Carette. Despite his attentions, the infection grew worse.

To the curé of Paris's Church of the Madeleine, Lully's perilous state presented the opportunity to further the Catholic church's campaign to ban opera. He advised Lully that his salvation called for throwing his latest opera into the fire. The composer agreed reluctantly to the sacrifice, and as the curé performed last rites, *Achille et Polyxène* went up in flames.

The prospect of salvation was apparently good for Lully's health, since over the next few days the swelling in his leg subsided. The marquis de Carette, seizing the credit, proudly declared Lully saved. The prince de Comti visited Lully and expressed horror that the composer had consented to the destruction of his new opera. "Quiet, quiet, monseigneur," the composer replied. "I knew perfectly well what I was doing—I have a second copy."

Some people might say that Lully was punished for his operatic duplicity. On March 22, he died at the age of fifty-four. □

Twin Fates

Chang and Eng Bunker, whose celebrity gave the English language the term Siamese twins, had no choice but to live together for sixty-two years. Nor had they any choice but to die together—or nearly so. They expired within three hours of each other on January 17, 1874.

Born in 1811 to a fisherman and his wife in Thailand, then the kingdom of Siam, the boys were joined at the chest by a short, tubular band of flesh. Doctors feared that separating them would prove fatal. Physicians today think that the brothers shared no vital organs, and had they lived a century later, surgical separation would have been a simple matter.

As it was, the conjoined brothers learned to manage quite well. As they grew, their fleshy bond stretched to the point that Chang and Eng could stand side by side. They swam, ran, and hiked, often covering eight to ten miles in a day, and were both excellent marksmen.

In 1829, an American sea captain and a British merchant in Bangkok learned of the twins' existence and conceived a plan to exhibit them. There began a ten-year-long career during which the twins astonished crowds in America and Europe. They made enough money to retire to a tobacco farm near Mount Airy, North Carolina. There they became United States citizens, adopted the name Bunker, and in 1843 married two sisters. They sired a total of twenty-one children.

Because the Bunkers' farm was ravaged during the Civil War, they made a European tour in 1870 in order to raise money to restore it. Returning to America after this tour, Chang, always the frailer

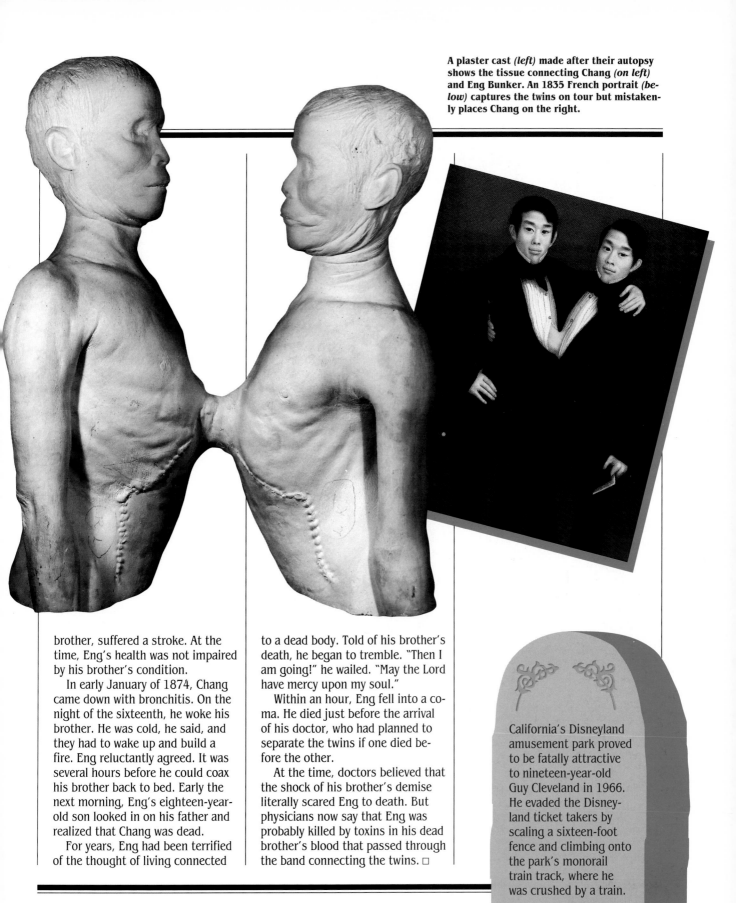

A plaster cast *(left)* made after their autopsy shows the tissue connecting Chang *(on left)* and Eng Bunker. An 1835 French portrait *(below)* captures the twins on tour but mistakenly places Chang on the right.

brother, suffered a stroke. At the time, Eng's health was not impaired by his brother's condition.

In early January of 1874, Chang came down with bronchitis. On the night of the sixteenth, he woke his brother. He was cold, he said, and they had to wake up and build a fire. Eng reluctantly agreed. It was several hours before he could coax his brother back to bed. Early the next morning, Eng's eighteen-year-old son looked in on his father and realized that Chang was dead.

For years, Eng had been terrified of the thought of living connected to a dead body. Told of his brother's death, he began to tremble. "Then I am going!" he wailed. "May the Lord have mercy upon my soul."

Within an hour, Eng fell into a coma. He died just before the arrival of his doctor, who had planned to separate the twins if one died before the other.

At the time, doctors believed that the shock of his brother's demise literally scared Eng to death. But physicians now say that Eng was probably killed by toxins in his dead brother's blood that passed through the band connecting the twins. □

California's Disneyland amusement park proved to be fatally attractive to nineteen-year-old Guy Cleveland in 1966. He evaded the Disneyland ticket takers by scaling a sixteen-foot fence and climbing onto the park's monorail train track, where he was crushed by a train.

Sweet Death

Until the evening of April 23, 1974, Carl Barnett had never conducted a public performance of J. S. Bach's "Come, Sweet Death." Thus he was a bit edgy as he stepped on stage at Will Rogers High School in Tulsa, Oklahoma, but he mustered his nerve, lifted his baton, and the seventy-five-member student orchestra began its performance.

In the midst of the piece, however, the fifty-nine-year-old director suddenly clutched his chest and fell forward, toppling a music stand. A nurse in the audience leaped onto the stage, and two members of the orchestra attempted heart massage, but their efforts proved to be in vain. Sweet death, in the form of a heart attack, had come for conductor Carl Barnett. □

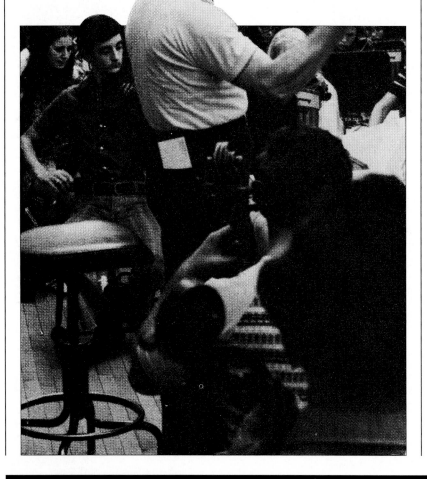

Director Carl Barnett conducts a rehearsal of the Will Rogers High School orchestra the year before his sudden death on the podium.

Beyond Boredom

For more than three decades, organic food guru Jerome I. Rodale assiduously promoted his belief that a special diet and other practices would prolong human life. Jerome Rodale was no obscure crackpot; his message found wide acceptance in the readership of two popular magazines that he published, *Organic Gardening and Farming* and *Prevention.*

Vigorous and exuberant at the age of seventy-two, the bearded Rodale followed a daily regimen that included seventy food supplements and ten to twenty minutes under a machine that emitted radio waves. The waves, he said, boosted the body's supply of electricity. Rodale believed that wheat was terrible for people and sugar was worse. Nevertheless, he occasionally gave in to a dish of ice cream.

Rodale was a tireless advocate for his publications and beliefs and not above a bit of hyperbole. "I'm going to live to be 100, unless I'm run down by a sugar-crazed taxi driver," he said in a *New York Times Magazine* profile on June 6, 1971. The next day the publisher arrived in Manhattan for a taping of Dick Cavett's popular television talk show. "I'm in great shape," Rodale told Cavett as the cameras rolled. "I could get up

Organic food promoter Jerome Rodale tastes sunflower seeds at his Pennsylvania farm in 1970.

line from you exhilarates my spirits and gives me a glow of pleasure."

By the spring of 1826, it was apparent that both John Adams, at ninety, and Thomas Jefferson, at eighty-three, were nearing the end of their lives, and by early summer both men were bedridden. On July 4, Adams woke briefly at dawn. "It's a great day!" he exclaimed. "It's a good day! Independence forever!" He went back to sleep, then woke and uttered his last words: "Thomas Jefferson survives." He died shortly before sunset.

In fact, Adams had outlived his old friend from Virginia. Jefferson was determined to see the Glorious Fourth, but he was sinking fast. On the evening of July 3, he roused himself. "Is it the Fourth?" he asked. He dozed again and died the next morning. □

Correct Departure

Since the 1600s, when the newly founded Académie Française issued the first dictionary of the French language, France has guarded the purity of its tongue.

No modern Frenchman, however, has matched the punctiliousness of Dominique Bouhours *(right)*, a Jesuit educator and critic who translated the New Testament into French.

Bouhours, who died in 1702 at the age of seventy-four, was a grammarian to the end. As he breathed his last, Bouhours said, "I am about to, or I am going to die. Both expressions are used." □

Parting Shot

Uncle John was the fond nickname his troops gave General John Sedgwick. A highly regarded and much-beloved Union officer during the Civil War, a West Point graduate, and the grandson of a Revolutionary War officer, Sedgwick, commander of the army's Sixth Corps, prepared for the Battle of Spotsylvania, in Virginia, early in 1864.

On the morning of May 9, Sedgwick was directing the placement of artillery when he noticed his soldiers ducking to avoid Confederate sharpshooters. Standing tall and unprotected, the general reassured his troops. "They couldn't hit an elephant at this distance," he asserted. With the soldiers only slightly reassured by their commander's braggadocio, the work continued.

The troops were correct in their caution. Before the morning was out, Sedgwick was shot in the face by a sniper's bullet, and he died not long after. □

Stunned officers attempt to aid Union general John Sedgwick, felled by a Confederate sniper during the Battle of Spotsylvania.

Court of the Damned

Whenever he pronounced the death sentence, it is alleged, Judge Isaac Parker *(below)* bowed his head and wept. If that statement is true, tears must have flowed freely in Parker's bailiwick, which became known as the Court of the Damned.

Between 1875, when he became federal judge for western Arkansas, until his own death in 1896, Parker sentenced 160 men and women to death. Half of them eluded the noose through appeals and presidential commutations. But the other half—some of them sent to the gallows six at a time—earned Parker his appellation as the Hanging Judge. Although he may not have always shed a tear, Parker took no pleasure in sentencing people to death. Duty made him do it, at the cost of great inner turmoil.

Parker was named to the bench by President Ulysses Grant after serving two terms as a congressman from the state of Missouri. He had little patience with the finer points of the law, putting more stock in the biblical notion of an eye for an eye. Parker's sympathy lay only with the crime victim.

"People have said that I am cruel," the judge once remarked in defending his harsh reputation, "but they do not understand how I am situated." Indeed, Parker's district was beyond the imagination of most Americans. It was one of the largest in the nation, at 74,000 square miles, and the most murderous. Fort Smith, a brutish frontier town, was the seat of the district. It encompassed the Indian Territory, a popular refuge for desperadoes. What little protection the Indians received from the law was accorded by Judge Parker.

In September of 1896, three new judicial districts were created, and the Indian Territory was removed from Parker's jurisdiction. The judge, who had been ailing, died two months later, at the age of fifty-eight. The event was greeted with jubilation in some quarters—notably the Fort Smith jail—and dismay in others. Hundreds of Indians came to his funeral, and the chief of the Creeks placed a wreath on the judge's grave.

To the end, Parker was sure of his course. "People have said to me, 'You are the judge who has hung so many men,'" he remarked in an interview with a reporter shortly before his death. Each time, he said, he would answer, "It is not I who has hung them. I never hung a man. It is the law." □

Death in an Epigram

"I summed up all systems in a phrase, and all existence in an epigram," wrote Oscar Wilde, and for most of his life, the approach won laurels for the brilliant Irish-born playwright and poet. Amid the sanctimony of Victorian England, Wilde lived on his prodigious, irreverent wit. Nor did it desert him before he died, in 1900, when he was just forty-six years old.

A natural apostle of the new cult of "art for art's sake," Wilde perfected his style as a dandified aesthete during his student days at Oxford University. He affected lilac shirts, knee breeches, and a languid air, and filled his rooms with peacock feathers and sunflowers. His talent for epigrams—displayed in the sparkling dialogue of such plays as *Lady Windermere's Fan* and *The Importance of Being Earnest*—made him the lion of London's literary salons.

Wilde married and fathered two children. But he also had many homosexual liaisons, and in Victorian England, such behavior was a criminal offense. In 1895, the marquess of Queensberry, an avid sportsman whose name now graces the rules for boxing, accused Wilde of seducing his son. Foolishly, Wilde sued Queensberry for criminal libel, and the marquess responded by charging the playwright with indecent behavior. In a sensational trial, Wilde was found guilty and sentenced to two years at hard labor.

During the time he spent in prison, Wilde wrote one of his greatest works, *De Profundis*, an apologia for his life. He also incurred in prison an injury that probably led to his death—in a fall, he struck his head on the stone floor and perforated an eardrum. After his release in 1897, the bankrupt and ailing Wilde took refuge in Paris, where he subsisted for his last two years on credit and the kindness of friends.

Although Wilde no longer wrote, he had not lost his talent for an elegant turn of phrase, and some of his last words were among his most memorable. Confronted with the need for a costly operation on his injured and now badly infected ear, he observed, "I am dying beyond my means." The operation failed to eradicate the infection. It spread to his brain, where it developed into a painful and ultimately fatal case of cerebral meningitis.

Wilde remained an aesthete to the end, summoning the energy to criticize the gaudy profusion of huge magenta flowers papering the walls of his rented room. "My wallpaper and I are fighting a duel to the death," he told a friend. "One or the other of us has to go." □

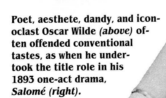

Poet, aesthete, dandy, and iconoclast Oscar Wilde *(above)* often offended conventional tastes, as when he undertook the title role in his 1893 one-act drama, *Salomé (right)*.

Fatal Flourish

With her lithe body, graceful movements, and diaphanous costumes, dancer Isadora Duncan captivated Europe in the early 1900s. At a time when dance was defined by ballet's tutus and toe shoes, she broke all of the rules with an artfully heedless grandeur. She died, at the age of forty-nine, with the same drama and panache that marked her life.

Raised in a bohemian household in San Francisco, Duncan was a free spirit. At six she organized a dancing school for other children in her neighborhood, and at ten she left school to become a professional dancer. But America was not ready for her unconventional art, and in 1900 she left for Europe to find the following she lacked at home.

Duncan threw herself into love affairs with the same abandon she showed onstage. Flaunting contemporary mores, she had two children by two different men, neither of whom did she marry. Romantically and artistically, she was at her peak in 1913, when tragedy struck with a vengeance: Her daughter and son were drowned when the car in which they were sitting accidentally rolled into the Seine. To relieve her sorrow, the bereaved Duncan became pregnant again as the result of a liaison with an Italian sculptor. The baby boy she bore died shortly after birth. Racked by grief, for three years she performed only dances of sorrow and withdrew from society.

In 1921, Duncan accepted an invitation to visit the newly established Soviet Union and there fell in love with Sergei Esenin, a poet seventeen years her junior who had suffered repeated bouts of madness. This time love led to marriage—bowing to convention made it easier to get Esenin a visa that would allow him to accompany her on a performing tour of the United States. The tour went badly—among other things, Duncan offended American sensibilities by baring her breasts. After the couple returned to Europe, they began to quarrel violently, and in 1924 Duncan and Esenin separated. A year later, he committed suicide.

Isadora Duncan's last years often found her penniless and blowzy from drink. But when her fortunes improved or romance was in the air, the old free spirit made a comeback. Perhaps on both scores, life seemed full of promise late in the summer of 1927. She was in Nice, where she was writing her memoirs for an American publisher. Dreaming of earning a handsome sum from her book, Duncan had been seized by the notion of buying a sporty Bugatti car.

The proprietor of the dealership, a handsome young former flying ace, was at least as attractive to Duncan as the car itself. They arranged to take it out for a trial spin on the evening of September 14. The weather was cool, and when the ace picked Duncan up at her dance studio he offered her his leather coat. Instead, she flung a long red silk shawl around her neck and stepped into the open car. With unknowing prescience Duncan bade a dramatic farewell: "Good-bye, my friends. I go to glory."

Duncan did not notice that her shawl was trailing outside the open car. As the Bugatti began to move forward, the shawl caught in the rear wheel. With a few quick revolutions, the shawl tightened and broke the dancer's neck. She died instantly. □

Isadora Duncan's unorthodox dance dress and choreography, seen in this publicity photo, echoed her flamboyant rejection of society's conventions.

A long-time teacher of hearing-impaired children, Alexander Graham Bell married one of his pupils, Mabel Hubbard, with whom he was photographed at their Cape Breton Island summer home in 1884.

A Sign before Dying

Alexander Graham Bell was born in 1847 into a Scots dynasty dedicated to the science of speech. His grandfather was an elocution professor, and his father pioneered Visible Speech, a system of illustrations depicting the position of throat, tongue, and lips for any sound. And although Bell himself is best known as the inventor of the telephone, he devoted much of his life to helping the deaf to speak.

It was Bell's inventive bent that enabled him to recognize that Visible Speech, although not designed as a teaching tool for deaf people, was ideal for that purpose. Thereafter, he used it in classes of deaf children in London and, after he immigrated to Boston in 1871, in the United States. One of his students, a young woman named Mabel Hubbard, became his wife.

Focusing his passion for invention on speech and sound, Bell produced, in addition to the telephone, an instrument called the audiometer that measures hearing acuity. He also devised improvements for the phonograph and the telegraph. The telephone made Bell wealthy, enabling him to finance other inventors' work as well as his own.

Unfortunately, Bell suffered from diabetes. In 1922, when he was at his summer estate on Cape Breton Island in Nova Scotia, the illness worsened. Experiments with insulin had scarcely begun, and there was no other effective treatment.

Throughout his life, the energetic Bell had been a voluble talker, his enthusiasms and views spilling out in a seldom-ceasing stream of speech. Now, however, the dying inventor was silent, even when his wife, Mabel, spoke to him and begged him not to leave her. "He turned and opened his eyes and smiled at me," Mabel wrote her daughter. "His fingers clasped mine with the old sign of 'No,' and whenever I called him to the very last he answered by that pressure."

North America marked Alexander Graham Bell's passing with silence. On the day that he was buried, telephone service throughout the United States and Canada was suspended for one minute. □

Death Wish

Carl Panzram started doing time in prison when he was eleven years old, and he died in prison at the age of thirty-nine. In the intervening years, by his own admission, he killed twenty-one people and sodomized more than 1,000 males. When he was finally sentenced to death for killing a prison worker in the federal penitentiary at Leavenworth, Kansas, in 1929, Panzram rejoiced at the prospect of the gallows and raged at the do-gooders who tried to have his sentence commuted. "I believe the only way to reform people is to kill 'em," Panzram wrote. "I hate the whole damned human race including myself." In a letter to President Herbert Hoover, he insisted on his "constitutional rights" to be hanged.

Panzram prepared the letter as a final appeal for death in case his execution was delayed. But he was never required to mail it, for on September 5, 1930, he got his wish. He helped the hangman, who had been brought in from Indiana, to fasten the leather harness used to restrain Panzram's arms. "Hurry it up, you Hoosier bastard!" Panzram snarled. "I could hang a dozen men while you're fooling around!"

Carl Panzram strode swiftly to the gallows, looked slowly around, spat twice, then raced up the steps to his death. □

Lost in Translation

Few last words were awaited more reverentially than those of Albert Einstein *(left)*. Long before his death in 1955 at the age of seventy-six, Einstein was widely recognized as the greatest scientist of the modern world. His wizened face and cloud of flyaway hair became for many the very image of genius. And although only a handful of people understood Einstein's contributions to science, such as the theory of relativity, his scientific eminence was unquestionable.

Born in Ulm, Germany, the little Einstein had not looked like a genius to his parents. He seemed so backward that they doubted his ability to make his way in the world. In fact, Einstein did not display his dazzling intellect for twenty-six years. Then, in the year of 1905, he burst onto the scientific scene with the publication of four breathtaking papers, each containing a new discovery: the first visible proof of the molecular constitution of matter, the equation of mass and energy, the general theory of relativity, and the foundation of the photon theory of light, for which he won the Nobel Prize in 1921.

Such brilliance was no shield against hate, however, and when Adolf Hitler came to power in 1932, Einstein, a Jew, left Germany to join the Institute for Advanced Studies in Princeton, New Jersey. There, for the rest of his life, he worked unsuccessfully on what he called the Unified Field Theory—a single set of laws that would explain all cosmic motion. His other quest, for world peace, was also a futile one.

Although he was a lifelong pacifist, in 1939 Einstein agreed to add his signature to a letter warning President Franklin Roosevelt that the Nazis might soon be able to set off a nuclear chain reaction and urging that the United States also develop a bomb. The result was the Manhattan Project, the destruction of the city of Hiroshima, and an atomic arms race that Einstein, horrified with what he had helped create, publicly condemned.

Far from relishing public debate, Einstein had a horror of the limelight, and as he aged, his desire to live and to die in obscurity grew stronger. He wanted no monument or grave, fearing that the site would become a public shrine. He insisted that his brain be used for research and his body be cremated; his ashes were to be scattered at an undisclosed place.

On April 17, 1955, Einstein was gravely ill in a Princeton hospital with an aneurysm in his aorta. He was in too much pain to work on his calculations, so he talked science and politics with his visitors. The talk was light, the patient seemed to be in good spirits, and the visitors left confident that he was improving. Around one o'clock the next morning, however, a night nurse noticed that Einstein's breathing had changed. She called in another nurse, and together they cranked up the head of the bed.

Einstein was muttering in German, his mother tongue, but a language totally foreign to the two women. Several minutes later, he was dead. The last words of Albert Einstein were lost forever. □

Her Favorite Things

Her best performances were all offstage, and actress Tallulah Bankhead *(right)* wrote her own best lines. "I'm as pure as the driven slush," was her comment about her love life. And when gossip columnist Earl Wilson had the temerity to ask the gravel-throated Tallulah, "Are you ever mistaken for a man on the phone?" she rasped, "No. Are you?"

The stunning daughter of wealthy Alabama Congressman and one-time Speaker of the House William Brockman Bankhead, Tallulah, as she was universally known, shone on stage in roles portraying characters scorning conventional standards of femininity. She was memorable as the predatory Regina Giddens in Lillian Hellman's *The Little Foxes* and the vixen Sabina in Thornton Wilder's *The Skin of Our Teeth.*

But Bankhead's fame was founded less on her thespian talents than on a reckless glamour and verve. She chain-smoked, drank, used cocaine, and cursed like a longshoreman while romping through scores of movie flops and the rare hit. Her sultry and stagily Southern trademark greeting—"Daaahling!"—be-

came part of the national lexicon.

In the end, Tallulah succumbed to the booze and drugs that had buoyed her in earlier years. Already afflicted with emphysema, in December 1968, at the age of sixty-six, the actress was hospitalized with a bad case of influenza. Psychotic behavior had become frequent, and Tallulah screamed about her hospital gown and tore the intravenous needles out of her arm. Pneumonia set in. Put on a respirator, she still struggled to talk. Tallulah's last discernible words were "codeine . . . bourbon." □

Let's Cool It

Harlem's Audubon Ballroom was packed by the time Malcolm X entered on the bright Sunday afternoon of February 21, 1965. He had just exchanged traditional Muslim greetings of peace with the crowd when a fracas broke out—a man seated several rows from the stage was accusing another of picking his pocket. "Hold it!" Malcolm said. "Don't get excited. Let's cool it, brothers!" As if on cue, three men with guns rushed the stage and blasted Malcolm at point-blank range. He was dead at thirty-nine years of age.

In a sense, the black leader's last words were an ironic coda to his life. After more than a decade as a vitriolic spokesman for the militant Black Muslim movement, Malcolm had recently moderated his views about "white devils" and embarked on a more moderate course. Whether or not the Black Muslim organization itself was responsible for his assassination—two of the men convicted of the crime were members of the movement—Malcolm paid a fatal price for urging peace among his brothers.

Born Malcolm Little in Omaha, Nebraska, he had been a likely recruit to militancy. His father was a minister who championed the cause of black nationalism, and white racists repeatedly threatened the family. The Reverend Little was run over by a streetcar and killed when his son was six years old, and Malcolm always believed that his father had been murdered and afterward dumped on the streetcar tracks.

As a young man, Malcolm made his way to New York and Boston, where a career in petty crime landed him behind bars for the first time in 1946. He spent a total of six years in prison. It was there that Malcolm first studied the teachings of Black Muslim Elijah Muhammad, leader of the Chicago-based separatist Nation of Islam. Upon his release, he moved to Chicago and traded what he now viewed as his slave name for the simple surname X.

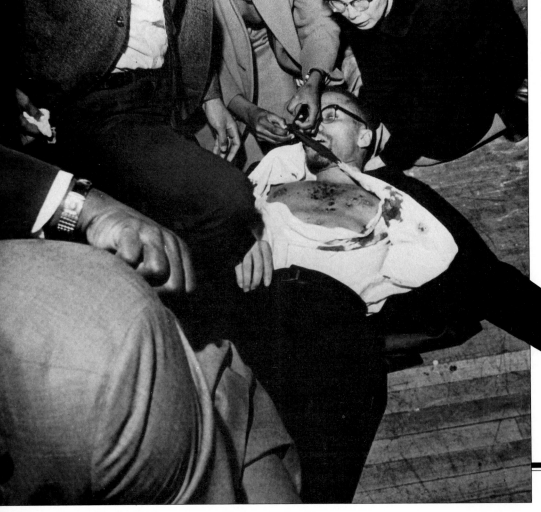

Moments after gunmen charged from the audience and unleashed a volley of shots at him, militant black leader Malcolm X lies dying on the stage of Harlem's Audubon Ballroom on February 21, 1965.

He was a spellbinding orator—a talent fostered by his other prison pastime, copying out the dictionary—and he quickly became a figure of such power that Muhammad's authority appeared in danger.

If Muhammad was looking for an excuse to unload Malcolm X, he found it in November of 1963, when Malcolm made an outrageous comment on the murder of President John F. Kennedy. It was a case of "the chickens coming home to roost," he declared. "Being an old farm boy myself, chickens coming home to roost never did make me sad; they've always made me glad."

Suspended from the Nation by Muhammad for his outburst, Malcolm established the rival Organization of Afro-American Unity, which focused more on black solidarity than on separatism. A pilgrimage to the holy city of Mecca and his travels through Africa deepened Malcolm's belief in Islam and inspired a concept of pan-Africanism that encompassed American blacks. And Malcolm made a startling reversal about whites, expressing the desire for "an honest white-black brotherhood."

Malcolm's relations with the Black Muslims became dangerously combative. In November 1964, he described himself as a marked man. "This thing with me will be resolved by death and violence." In February of 1965, his house in New York was firebombed. Malcolm blamed the Black Muslims, and they responded by accusing him of planting the bombs himself.

The violence did not end with the murder of Malcolm X. Hours after he had counseled his brothers to cool it, some of his infuriated followers firebombed two Black Muslim mosques. □

No Appeals

It had been a very bad night for the old woman, and the housekeeper caring for her was convinced she would not last the day. The attendant began to pray—first silently, then aloud. The woman lifted her head. "Damn it," muttered actress Joan Crawford, "don't you dare ask God to help me!" A few minutes later, she was dead.

Just why Crawford snapped at her caretaker's appeal for divine intercession may never be known. But it seems fair to say that her death on May 10, 1977, at the age of seventy-three brought an end to a tormented life.

The product of a broken home, Crawford reportedly performed menial chores to earn her way through private school where she endured broom-handle beatings from the headmaster's wife. Years later, as an adoptive mother, she repaid the beatings, with interest. In her memoir *Mommie Dearest*, Crawford's daughter Christina says that her mother inflicted beatings so vicious that she broke three hairbrushes across Christina's bottom before the child was five years old.

Toward the end of her life, Crawford returned to her former faith, Christian Science, and as a consequence she

Joan Crawford played a tough and self-sufficient career woman in the 1959 film *The Best of Everything*—a role she relished in real life, too.

stopped seeking medical attention. Her weight plummeting, perhaps because of an undiagnosed cancer, she spent her final months virtually alone, by her own choice a prisoner in her New York apartment. She passed her days watching television soap operas and declining all offers of help—familial, medical, and ultimately divine. □

Heroically portrayed by the nineteenth-century engraver Alfred James, Patrick Henry *(far right)* delivers his emotional plea for "liberty or death" to fellow Virginians.

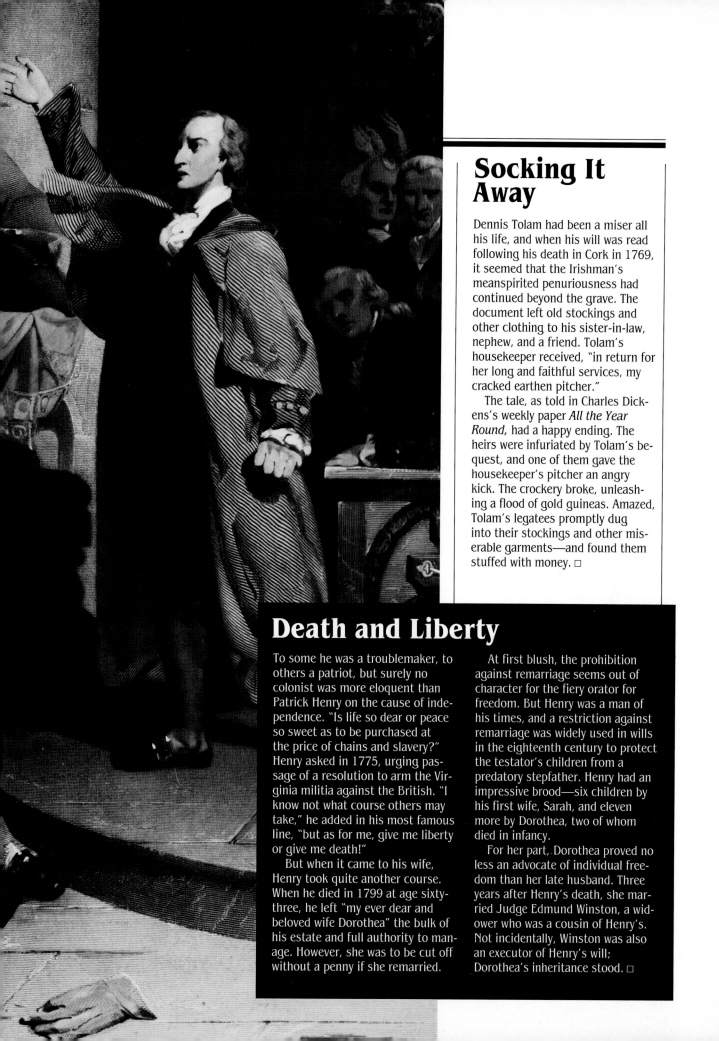

Socking It Away

Dennis Tolam had been a miser all his life, and when his will was read following his death in Cork in 1769, it seemed that the Irishman's meanspirited penuriousness had continued beyond the grave. The document left old stockings and other clothing to his sister-in-law, nephew, and a friend. Tolam's housekeeper received, "in return for her long and faithful services, my cracked earthen pitcher."

The tale, as told in Charles Dickens's weekly paper *All the Year Round,* had a happy ending. The heirs were infuriated by Tolam's bequest, and one of them gave the housekeeper's pitcher an angry kick. The crockery broke, unleashing a flood of gold guineas. Amazed, Tolam's legatees promptly dug into their stockings and other miserable garments—and found them stuffed with money. □

Death and Liberty

To some he was a troublemaker, to others a patriot, but surely no colonist was more eloquent than Patrick Henry on the cause of independence. "Is life so dear or peace so sweet as to be purchased at the price of chains and slavery?" Henry asked in 1775, urging passage of a resolution to arm the Virginia militia against the British. "I know not what course others may take," he added in his most famous line, "but as for me, give me liberty or give me death!"

But when it came to his wife, Henry took quite another course. When he died in 1799 at age sixty-three, he left "my ever dear and beloved wife Dorothea" the bulk of his estate and full authority to manage. However, she was to be cut off without a penny if she remarried.

At first blush, the prohibition against remarriage seems out of character for the fiery orator for freedom. But Henry was a man of his times, and a restriction against remarriage was widely used in wills in the eighteenth century to protect the testator's children from a predatory stepfather. Henry had an impressive brood—six children by his first wife, Sarah, and eleven more by Dorothea, two of whom died in infancy.

For her part, Dorothea proved no less an advocate of individual freedom than her late husband. Three years after Henry's death, she married Judge Edmund Winston, a widower who was a cousin of Henry's. Not incidentally, Winston was also an executor of Henry's will; Dorothea's inheritance stood. □

Grace Note

When Gary Mark Gilmore, a convicted double murderer, was shot by a Utah firing squad in 1977, he became the first person in a decade to be executed in the United States. As such, Gilmore was the focus of a legal debate in which, paradoxically, he and a large contingent of his supporters were on opposing sides. Foes of the death penalty fought all the way to the U.S. Supreme Court to keep him alive even though Gilmore himself insisted that he would rather die than serve more time in prison, and he greeted death with a grace that he had not shown in life.

Gilmore seemed headed for trouble almost from his birth in Texas in 1941. At twelve, he was sent to a home for juvenile delinquents, at fourteen he went to jail, and by the age of thirty-six, he had spent more than half of his life in one institution or another, much of it under maximum security. Gilmore was paroled from the federal penitentiary in Marion, Illinois, in April of 1976. Under the terms of his parole, he was to live and work for an uncle in Provo, Utah. By July, however, Gary Gilmore was back to his old ways. He robbed and murdered two men—a gas station attendant in Orem, Utah, and, the next night, a motel clerk in Provo.

The death sentence was handed down in October, but there were numerous legal delays. Gilmore grew impatient. He persuaded his twenty-year-old girlfriend, Nicole Barrett, to smuggle drugs to him so they could commit suicide on the same day. Both survived, and Gilmore made one more suicide attempt on his own. On January 17, 1977, he was at last allowed to take his seat before the firing squad. The warden asked if he had anything to say. "Let's do it," said Gilmore.

Those might have been Gilmore's last words. But before the command to fire could be given, a priest stepped forward to give the last rites. Surprising all, Gilmore stole his words. *Dominus vobiscum,* said Gilmore: The Lord be with you. *Et cum spiritu tuo,* answered the priest, giving the congregation's response: And with your spirit.

The priest stepped back, and Gary Gilmore got his last wish. □

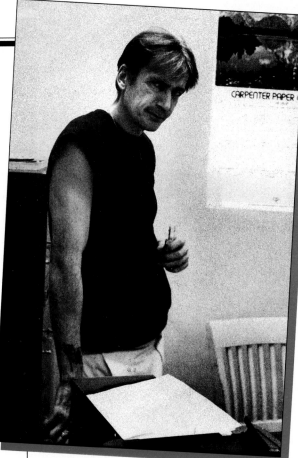

Murderer Gary Gilmore savors a swig of whiskey smuggled into prison by photographer Lawrence Schiller shortly before Gilmore's execution in 1977.

Widowed in the 1800s by a woman who was to receive an annuity "as long as she is above ground," a Major Hook of the British East India Company moved his late wife's remains into a room of their home and continued to receive her income for the rest of his life.

Ashes to Ashes

No one loved a good smoke better than a nineteenth-century Dutchman named Klaes, a wealthy linen merchant from Rotterdam. Known to acquaintances as the King of Smokers, Klaes is said to have smoked more than four tons of tobacco during his eighty years. When he died, around 1875, he left this world in a cloud of smoke.

In his will, Klaes directed that all the smokers in the Netherlands be invited to his funeral. Each was to be given ten pounds of tobacco and two pipes engraved with Klaes's name, coat of arms, and date of death. The local poor who attended the funeral would receive ten pounds of tobacco and a small cask of good beer on each anniversary of his death. All Klaes's mourners were to keep their pipes lit throughout the funeral, then empty the ashes onto the coffin.

The coffin itself was a monument to smoking. Klaes said it should be lined with the cedar from his old Havana cigar boxes, and that a box of French caporal and a packet of Dutch tobacco be placed at his feet. If there was smoking in the next world, Klaes wanted to be prepared. He had his favorite pipe placed at his side, along with a box of matches, a flint and steel, and some tinder—because, he said, there was no way of knowing how one lit one's pipe in the afterlife. □

Snuffed Out

Snuff taking was a popular habit two centuries ago, and mourners at wakes were sometimes invited to take a pinch of snuff from a dish inside the deceased's coffin. But for Margaret Thompson, a Londoner who died in 1777, a single dish of the pulverized tobacco was not enough. In her will, Thompson left orders for a funeral that was to be completely up to snuff.

Instead of flowers, the best Scotch snuff was to line her coffin and cover her remains, for "nothing can be so pleasant and refreshing to me, as that precious powder." The six men who bore her casket were to be great snuff takers, and they were to wear snuff-colored beaver hats. Six ladies carrying her coffin's pall were also to carry boxes of snuff "to take for their refreshment as they go along."

The minister was to sniff snuff as he walked before the casket, and Thompson's servant was to sprinkle snuff on the ground and among the crowd following the procession to the burial ground. At least two bushels of snuff were to be distributed at the door of Thompson's house. Every person attending the funeral service would be presented with a pound of the best Scotch snuff—according to its donor, "the grand cordial of human nature."

It is believed that Margaret Thompson's funeral instructions were carried out. □

Burning Passion

Wills have long been popular instruments of revenge for disappointed lovers, but probably none holds a candle to the testament left by a nineteenth-century lover who lost his mind after losing his amour. The story was told by a contemporary

British physician, Forbes Winslow. A specialist in the treatment of insanity, he said that he discovered the account in a French publication.

Bent on suicide, the jilted lover, Winslow reported, told his servant that he wanted his body to be boiled down, the fat extracted, and a candle made from it. The lighted candle was to be presented to his unfaithful former mistress.

The distraught suitor then wrote a letter in which he told his lady love that he had long burned for her—and was burning even as she read his words. According to Winslow, the request was carried out. □

The Odd Couple

Phineas T. Barnum and Henry Bergh were natural adversaries. As proprietor of the Greatest Show on Earth—a combination circus, zoo, and freak show—Barnum made a fortune exploiting everyone and everything he could. As founder of the American Society for the Prevention of Cruelty to Animals and president of its New York chapter, Bergh was determined to prevent Barnum from exploiting dumb animals.

For the better part of two decades, the two men hurled epithets at each other: Bergh was a "miserable pettyfogger" and Barnum a "semi-barbarian." Yet the pair also enjoyed a symbiotic relationship. Their battles helped publicize their respective activities, and eventually they became great friends.

A serpent was the subject of Barnum and Bergh's first skirmish. In

1866, the year the ASPCA was chartered in New York, Bergh threatened legal action when he learned that a boa constrictor in Barnum's menagerie was being fed live rabbits in full public view. To avoid trouble, two Barnum employees transported the snake across the Hudson River to a hotel room in Jersey City, New Jersey, for its dinner. But Henry Bergh was not to be easily mollified. Raging against his enemy's "atrocity," he charged, "Barnum sends his serpents over to Hoboken to feed on live animals." Bergh might have simply confused the location of the boa constrictor's refuge, but it is more likely that dragging Hoboken into the affair was meant to malign Barnum. Jersey City's saloon-ridden next-door neighbor, Hoboken was considered a haven for seamen, prostitutes,

and other unsavory characters.

Where another man might have feared scandal, Barnum smelled publicity. Bergh, too, probably recognized the opportunity for a good headline when he saw it. Barnum obtained a letter of support from Louis Agassiz, a prominent zoologist at Harvard University, and vowed to send their correspondence to the newspapers unless Bergh recanted. Bergh retorted by labeling the showman "an adept in the school of humbug." Although Barnum had more than once styled himself the Prince of Humbugs, he claimed to be outraged by Bergh's language. It betrayed "low breeding and a surplus of self-conceit," he sniffed, adding, "Your dictatorial air is unsufferable."

After the noisy airing of their differences, the two men struck a compromise: The boa constrictor would be fed in New York, after hours, with no spectators. The dinner would still be live, but public morals would be protected.

Over the years, Barnum and Bergh enjoyed their skirmishes. In 1880, they knocked heads resoundingly over a new Barnum & Bailey act in which a horse named Salamander was to jump through a series of blazing hoops. On the first night, an attendant let one of the hoops slip, and Salamander reportedly ran off with his mane and tail on fire. When Bergh de-

manded an end to the "barbarity," Barnum replied that it was no such thing and invited Bergh and the press to see for themselves. When the act was next performed, Barnum himself jumped through the fiery hoops with the horse bringing up the rear. The ASPCA meekly withdrew its objection.

But by this time, the foes had become friends. Barnum had helped found a chapter of the ASPCA in Bridgeport, Connecticut, where he lived, and a few weeks before the Salamander fracas, Bergh recommended Barnum for the new chapter's board. And when a newspaper criticized the treatment of Barnum circus elephants in 1885, Bergh defended the showman as "one of the most humane and kind-hearted men living."

In their declining years, Bergh proposed to Barnum that he remember in his will "the poor dumb animals from whom he has derived so large a share of his splendid fortune." One of the mourners at Bergh's funeral in 1888, Barnum took his friend's suggestion to heart. He died three years later at the age of seventy-nine, leaving a $1,000 bequest to the New York ASPCA. Barnum's will also honored Bergh himself with a donation of $1,000 to Bridgeport for a statue of the animal lover. Instead of a statue, the city of Bridgeport memorialized Bergh with a drinking fountain for horses. □

No Preservatives

There were few things that Brooklyn physician Thomas Holmes (*overleaf*) liked better than a good corpse. Even in medical school, he had shown a peculiar interest in the condition of the cadavers he studied, and his preference for practicing on the dead continued after he hung out his shingle. Preserving the dead fascinated Holmes, and he came to claim the title—with more hyperbole than accuracy—of "originator of embalming in United States." Oddly enough, however, Holmes's dying wish was that he be buried unembalmed.

In the mid-nineteenth century, undertakers were most often furniture makers and thus more concerned with building the casket than handling the corpse. Embalming was uncommon, and most bodies were hurried into the ground before they decomposed. Around 1850, Holmes took it upon himself to popularize the process and enrich himself in the bargain. He was then working as a coroner's physician, and he began by experimenting with the bodies that came his way. Displaying a fine instinct for self-promotion, he exhibited one of his embalmed corpses at an undertaker's. The press was alerted and, Holmes wrote later, "thousands went to see the body." Several years later the physician-entrepreneur opened a drugstore. Two of the featured products were a homemade embalming fluid that, Holmes claimed, needed only to be wiped on a corpse to preserve it, and a root beer that he made in his cellar.

When the Civil War broke out, Holmes volunteered—not as a ◊

Built with money from showman P. T. Barnum, a drinking fountain for horses in Bridgeport, Connecticut, memorializes Barnum's friendly nemesis Henry Bergh, a pioneer protector of animals.

soldier but as an embalmer of the Union dead. Holmes later boasted that during the war he had embalmed 4,028 "officers and soldiers, most of them on Southern battlefields, in the hottest weather."

He also obtained at least five patents in the field of embalming. Four were for mundane items like pumps and chemicals. The fifth was granted for a pouch of rubberized canvas called the Eureka. Intended primarily as a body bag for storing the battlefield dead, the Eureka was a wonderfully versatile device. Its inventor also touted it as a sleeping bag, a stretcher, and, in cases of hurried retreat across water, an inflatable raft, with eight handles that could be gripped by survivors.

When the war ended, Holmes went back to running his pharmacy and pursuing experiments in embalming. For a time an especially impressive piece of his handiwork— the well-preserved head and shoulders of a fourteen-year-old girl—held a place of honor in the window of the pharmacy. He developed a fluid that gave bodies a stony hardness. After Holmes's death, a few petrified corpses were unearthed in his cellar. No wrongdoing was alleged, however, because authorities found signed releases allowing him to experiment on the corpses.

Holmes's own end began in 1896, when he fell twelve feet from a ladder and landed on his head. Although he survived the accident, he soon began experiencing psychotic episodes. He was hospitalized after chopping up the household furniture and threatening his wife with an ax. When he died in 1900 at the age of eighty-three, Holmes made headlines. One obituary proclaimed, "Dead Embalmer Wants NO Embalming!" His wish was carried out. □

The Petticoat Will

The old man was on his deathbed in a Los Angeles, California, nursing home, so when he told the nurse that he wanted to write his will, it was only natural for her to oblige him. Lillian Pelkey hiked up her skirt and took down George Hazeltine's instructions on her white voile petticoat: $10,000 to her;

$10,000 to the proprietor of the nursing home, Madeline Higgins; and the balance of his estate to his grandniece. Later that day, March 15, 1925, the eighty-six-year-old Hazeltine died.

So went the tale told by Pelkey

and Higgins when, three months later, they offered the petticoat for probate. In a will written in 1919, however, Hazeltine had left $10,000 to each of his two lawyers, Frank

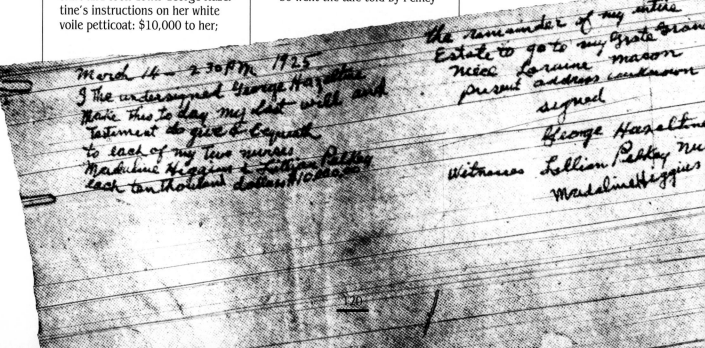

Hutton and Dell Schweitzer. One dollar was to go to the old man's grandniece, Lorraine Moody Richmond, and the balance of the estate was to be put in trust, with Dell Schweitzer as its manager, for the benefit of Hazeltine's sister and his sister-in-law. George Hazeltine's estate was appraised at more than $200,000—an amount well worth fighting for, and the case of the petticoat will went to trial.

The unconventional will was upheld, but California law barred Pelkey and Higgins from receiving their bequests because they were witnesses to the document. Richmond was almost home free, but lawyers Hutton and Schweitzer declared their intention to appeal the court's decision to throw out the 1919 will. In order to avoid a long and expensive legal wrangle, Richmond sold them a substantial interest in the estate.

The case was not yet over, however. Pelkey and Higgins went to court with the claim that Richmond had reneged on an agreement to give each of them $10,000 in exchange for their promise not to sue her. Richmond, the plaintiffs said, had given them the slip—they received only $2,000. The court ruled the arrangement invalid and dismissed their suit. □

Duly dated, signed, and witnessed, George Hazeltine's brief deathbed will was written on the hem of nurse Lillian Pelkey's petticoat.

Double Standard

Whenever T. M. Zink *(below)* ranted about women, which was often, he would reassure his wife, "Of course, you know I don't mean you, Ida." Zink, a lawyer in Le Mars, Iowa, died in 1930 at the age of seventy-two, leaving a will in which he attempted to justify his view of the opposite sex. "My intense hatred of women is not of recent origin, or development, nor based upon any personal differences I ever had with them," he explained, "but is the result of my experiences with women, observations of them, and study of all literatures and philosophical works."

In order to perpetuate his misogyny, Zink bequeathed his $80,000 estate to Le Mars for building a library. Several stringent conditions were attached. Men over the age of forty would select the reading materials, and all of the library's books, as well as any works of art and decorations on the premises, must be by men. "No Woman Admitted" was to be carved in stone over each door, and if any female was allowed to enter, the trust Zink established would be revoked and the library transferred to another Iowa town willing to meet the will's conditions.

T. M. Zink had a sweeping vision of a library "in which all known human knowledge may be found, by any man wishing the same." No book was to be excluded "on account of any the-

ory, philosophy, ethics, religion, or language"—unless, of course, its author was female.

Why Zink hated women so much is unclear. Ida Zink was his second wife—he had been widowed at fifty-two—and his newspaper obituary described their union as "ideally happy." Despite their supposed happiness, however, Zink's sole bequest to his widow was the option to rent their house for forty dollars a month. He left his stepdaughter five dollars.

The stepdaughter contested the will—a move that presumably would not have surprised Zink in view of his low opinion of women. The court upheld her challenge and rejected Zink's will. Over his dead body, his stepdaughter received her just inheritance. □

Big Daddy

Charles Vance Millar, a prominent Toronto lawyer, was a model of rectitude until his sudden death from a heart attack in 1926, at the age of seventy-three, in his office on a Sunday afternoon. But Charles Millar had always harbored a perverse sense of fun, and his best jokes turned on money and greed. It amused Millar, for instance, to place a one-dollar bill on the sidewalk and watch the expressions of passersby as they pocketed it.

In death, Millar remained a joker, but on a grander scale. The instrument for carrying out his final exploits—fitting for a lawyer—was his last will and testament. With one bequest, he outraged guardians of public morals, set off a nationwide melodrama, and encouraged the birth of at least 100 babies.

The majority of his grants merely tweaked the noses of Toronto's citizenry. He left shares in the Ontario Jockey Club to a government official and a clergyman who were vociferous opponents of racetrack betting. To three lawyer friends who had nothing in common, Millar left his vacation home in Jamaica—presumably in the hopes it would lead to open warfare. The joke turned sour when the heirs learned that their supposed benefactor had actually sold the house two years before.

Millar left the best for last. In the final clause of his will, the lawyer bequeathed the bulk of his considerable estate to the mother who would, in the decade after his death, give birth in Toronto to the greatest number of children. That bequest set off what became known as the Great Stork Derby, an event that for years caught the world's attention.

Millar's relatives challenged the will, arguing that it violated the public interest by encouraging women to have too many children too soon, and to have them out of wedlock—a point that the will itself did not address. The will was upheld. "I don't see that reproduction of the human race is contrary to public morals," said Justice William Edward Middleton, himself one of nine children.

As the Stork Derby's deadline approached, more than a dozen women claimed to be the winner, and Middleton was called upon to exercise the wisdom of Solomon. Should stillborn children count? Illegitimate children?

In the end, four women, with nine children apiece born during that decade,

Posing here with fourteen of their sixteen children, Lucy and Arthur Timleck *(far right)* produced nine offspring during Toronto's Stork Derby and shared the contest's top prize with three other couples.

divided the prize. Each received $125,000, more than many Canadians at that time would earn in a lifetime. Two other mothers, their tallies reduced by illegitimate and stillborn children, were declared runners-up, sharing a consolation prize of $25,000.

The money was welcome to all, and so, presumably, were the offspring. Nevertheless, Lucy Timleck, one of the championship mothers, confessed after the derby's conclusion that her dearest wish was to work for birth control. □

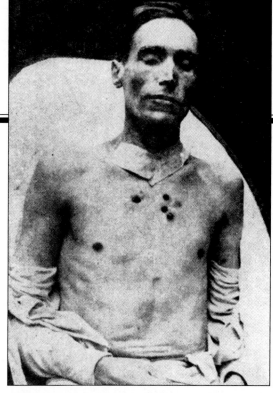

An official photographer recorded the bullet holes in the body of labor organizer Joe Hill shortly after his 1915 execution.

Blowin' in the Wind

Joe Hill was a political radical and labor organizer in the early years of the twentieth century. He became a martyr when western business interests and government officials conspired to have him tried on a trumped-up murder charge. He was convicted, and in Salt Lake City in 1915, he was put to death.

By the time of his execution by firing squad at the age of thirty-six, Hill was already legendary for his words and deeds. The songs he wrote were sung in union halls and picket lines throughout the world. His last words were characteristically stirring. "I'll show you how to die," he told his executioners. "My conscience is clear."

He left a rhyming will that exhorted unionists to "Let the merry breezes blow / My dust to where some flowers grow. / Perhaps some fading flower then / Would come to life and bloom again."

His union, the then large and far-flung Industrial Workers of the World, or Wobblies, saw to it that a fragment of Hill would rest in vir-

tually every corner of the world.

In his last letter from prison, Hill had urged the Wobblies, "Don't mourn, organize." Nonetheless, thousands did mourn. The union held a funeral in Salt Lake City, then shipped the body to Chicago for a second service. Thronging the streets in Chicago, mourners halted traffic for blocks, singing Hill's songs as they inched along with his hearse to the cemetery.

After eulogies were delivered in nine languages, the union had his body cremated and sent packets of the ashes to IWW locals in every state except Utah and to sympathetic groups on every continent except Antarctica. The envelopes bore the legend, "Joe Hill, Murdered by the Capitalist Class, November 19, 1915. Industrial Workers of the World. We Never Forget." The contents of all but two packets were released on May 1, 1916.

One of the stray packets was lost when thugs raided and wrecked an IWW hall in Toledo, Ohio. But union member George Carey recovered ◊

the ashes in 1919, keeping the envelope until a summer day in 1950, when he decided that "I was grown old and I had an obligation to carry out." Carey scattered the remains in his garden, "with no more ceremony than a murmured 'Goodbye, Joe.'"

One other packet surfaced more than sixty years after Hill's death. Inexplicably omitted from the 1916 scattering, the packet had been mailed in 1917 from IWW headquarters in Chicago but was intercepted by the Post Office, labeled possibly subversive, and sent to the Bureau of Investigation in Washington under the Espionage Act. All such items were entrusted to the National Archives in 1944 and eventually catalogued. In 1988, a court determined that Joe Hill's ashes did not constitute a federal record, and the remains were handed over to Frederic Lee, an IWW official. The newfound bits of Joe Hill's remains were mixed with sand, distributed to union offices, and scattered in several states. The final grains were tossed to the wind at the 1990 International Labor conference in Stockholm, Sweden. □

An English farmer, believing his death would only begin a thirty-year sleep, directed that his coffin be hung in the barn and the lid fixed to ease his exit on awakening. His wishes were followed when he died in 1721. Thirty years later, still in his eternal nap, he was buried.

Sole Support

Conrad Cantzen *(below)* was a familiar sight along Broadway. He was an actor, but he rarely got the bit parts he sought. More often, he panhandled. When he died, at the age of seventy-eight in 1945, Cantzen left a will that contained a curiously fitting bequest. To the surprise of all—including the Actors' Fund, which paid for the supposedly penniless Cantzen's funeral—he also left a handsome sum to carry it out.

The will established the Conrad Cantzen Shoe Fund for impoverished actors. "Many times I have been on my uppers," Cantzen recalled in his will, "and the thinner the soles of my shoes were, the less courage I had to face the managers in looking for a job." The bequest was funded with $226,000 worth of savings accounts, government bonds, and gilt-edge securities.

Since then, the Cantzen Shoe Fund has shod thousands of theater people down on their luck—in an ordinary month, it gives money to between twenty and thirty down-at-the-heels actors. All a beneficiary needs is a membership card in a professional theatrical union and a receipt for the shoes. If the pair costs no more than eighty dollars, the fund will hand over forty dollars or the full price of the shoes, whichever is less. Lest certain thespians be encouraged to extravagance, no reimbursement is made for a pair of shoes costing more than eighty dollars.

Enjoying Cantzen's largess is not a one-time thing. An individual can dip into the fund once a year, indefinitely, and go job-hunting with new shoes and new courage, courtesy of Conrad Cantzen. □

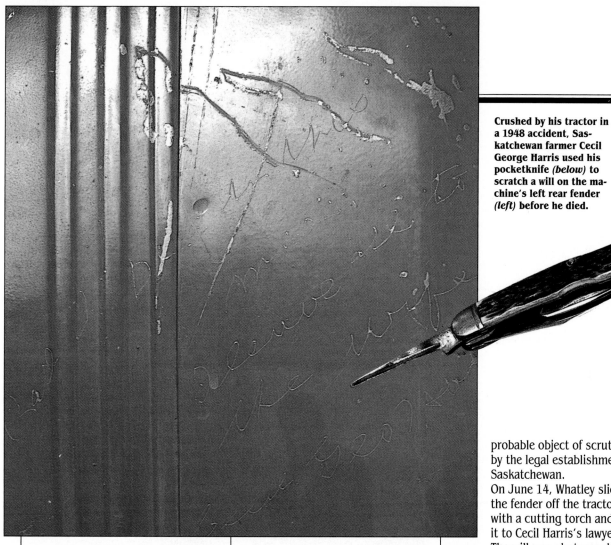

Crushed by his tractor in a 1948 accident, Saskatchewan farmer Cecil George Harris used his pocketknife *(below)* to scratch a will on the machine's left rear fender *(left)* before he died.

Fender Bender

It was just past noon on June 8, 1948, and Cecil George Harris, a Saskatchewan farmer, was working alone in the southwest quarter of his grain fields. He was adjusting the disk apparatus on his plow when his tractor suddenly lurched backward, pinning Harris between tractor and plow. His left leg, caught under the tractor's left rear wheel, bled profusely. No amount of effort by Harris could move the machinery off him.

But Harris's hands were free and his mind was clear, so with his pocketknife he scratched his will into a fender of his tractor. "In case I die in this mess," Harris wrote, "I leave all to the wife."

Harris's wife, Bessie May, found her husband in the field later that night. A neighbor, George Whatley, helped pull the farmer out from under his equipment and take him to a hospital. Harris died on June 10.

That morning, as Whatley and a friend, Louis Large, were spreading insecticide on Harris's fields, they paused to examine the dead man's tractor, which was still parked at the scene of the accident. It was Large who discovered the writing on the fender and pointed it out to Whatley. Whatley showed it to the widow, and for the next few days, the fender became the im-

probable object of scrutiny by the legal establishment of Saskatchewan.

On June 14, Whatley sliced the fender off the tractor with a cutting torch and took it to Cecil Harris's lawyer.

The will was photographed, and Whatley, Large, and several other witnesses signed affidavits about the condition of the fender. Mrs. Harris, along with a bank manager and the lawyer, confirmed that the signature on the fender was indeed her late husband's.

About a month after Cecil Harris's gruesome accident, the fender was admitted to probate. Although his sister contested the will, the fender proved as robust legally as it was mechanically: Bessie May Harris received all of the property, and the fender was filed, among hundreds of more conventional wills, in a basement at the Surrogate Court in the District of Kerrobert, Saskatchewan. □

Spelling Lesson

Playwright George Bernard Shaw hated the standard alphabet with a passion. A dabbler in phonetics and spelling from his boyhood days in Dublin on, Shaw concluded that twenty-six letters was a woefully inadequate number to represent the sounds of the English language. Some letters—*A, E, I, O,* and *U,* for instance—had to do double or triple duty, while *C* and *Q* worthlessly duplicated the sounds of the more useful *S, K,* and *W.* Because the alphabet was not phonetic, English spelling was irrational and inefficient—"alfabet" was, to Shaw's way of thinking, a great improvement on convention. Moreover, a new set of symbols would boost literary output. If Shakespeare and Dickens had not needed to laboriously write out silent *E*'s and other unnecessary letters, Shaw noted, they might "have written two or three more plays and novels than they had time to get through."

Phonetics cropped up in Shaw's 1913 play *Pygmalion,* in which the irascible professor Henry Higgins teaches flower girl Eliza Doolittle to exchange her Cockney accent for the elegant speech of a duchess. Neither the play—which inspired the Broadway hit *My Fair Lady*— nor Shaw's other lobbying efforts advanced his linguistic notions. But he was no quitter. A gadfly by nature, Shaw was prepared to back reform with money if words did not work, and when he died in 1950 at the age of ninety-four, he willed most of his estate to the cause of alphabetical innovation.

Although Shaw had during his long alphabetical advocacy proposed various improvements, his will left it to experts to devise a new system. He specified only that it should consist of at least forty letters, sixteen of them vowels. Each sound would be represented by a single letter, and pronunciation would be based on the recorded broadcasts of the late British king George V, whose voice and delivery the playwright had greatly admired. Shaw also asked that his play *Androcles and the Lion* be printed in the old and the new alphabets and that copies be sent to the world's major libraries.

Ruling that Shaw's bequest was too vague, the courts turned the money over to his ultimate beneficiaries—the British Museum, the Royal Academy of Dramatic Art, and the National Gallery of Ireland. These institutions did, however, partially execute Shaw's will by sponsoring a competition for a phonetic alphabet. Four winners were chosen, and *Androcles and the Lion* was translated into one of the victorious entries. But the exercise cost only a pittance, and it produced no practical results. Shaw had fought the good fight—and lost. □

In his 1950 will, British playwright George Bernard Shaw *(left)* directed scholars to create a new English alphabet and publish a bi-alphabetical edition of his play *Androcles and the Lion (below)* to demonstrate the new scheme's value.

ANDROCLES AND THE LION

an appalling roar. Androcles crouches and hides his face in his hands. The lion gathers himself for a spring, swishing his tail to and fro through the dust in an ecstasy of anticipation. Androcles throws up his hands in supplication to heaven. The lion checks at the sight of Androcles's face. He then steals towards him; smells him; arches his back; purrs like a motor car; finally rubs himself against Androcles, knocking him over. Androcles, supporting himself on wrist, looks affrightedly at the li limps on three paws, holding up t it was wounded. A flash of r up the face of A

The Lady and the Tramps

As a child, Eleanor Ritchey *(above)*, the heiress to the Quaker State Refining Corporation, had always wanted a dog. She never got one until she grew up—and then she went dog crazy. By the time she died in 1968 at the age of fifty-eight, Ritchey owned 150 dogs, most of them mongrels. She named them the beneficiaries of practically all of her four-million-dollar estate. It included a 192-acre ranch in Florida where, Ritchey directed, the lucky dogs were to live out their natural lives. When the last one died or was adopted, the estate was to go to veterinary research.

Ritchey was apparently living sans dogs in Fort Lauderdale when a chance meeting with dog lover Mark Strong, the janitor at Ritchey's bank and the owner of fifteen cocker spaniels, changed her life. Strong's enthusiasm for canines was contagious. Ritchey hired him as her chauffeur and assistant. One of his prime responsibilities was to help her collect strays. With Strong driving and Ritchey riding in back with open cans of dog food, the pair cruised the streets of south Florida in her Cadillac, picking up mutts. At one time, as many as fifty dogs lived in Ritchey's small house and a half-dozen slept in her bed. None was housebroken.

After a time, Ritchey realized that the house could not hold her growing brood. She bought a twelve-acre property to accommodate the dogs but chose not to move in with them. The neighbors complained so bitterly about the odor and incessant barking that Ritchey eventually bought the ranch near Deerfield Beach. The dogs had been installed there for close to a year when Ritchey died on October 14, 1968.

A dog's life on the Ritchey ranch was a mixed blessing. The bank that was trustee for the estate lavished a fortune each year on the mutts—$17,000 for food and housing and $12,000 for weekly medical check-ups and drugs such as special vitamin and mineral supplements, eye salve, and ear drops. Because Ritchey opposed euthanasia even for dogs suffering serious and painful illnesses, surgery was performed to save the sickest ones.

The ranch was periodically threatened by people who felt the money might be better spent on two-legged beings, and it had to be defended by barbed wire and around-the-clock guards. The dogs were tattooed to prove their membership in the original 150, segregated by sex to prevent the production of a new generation of heirs, and confined to ten-foot runways in front of their kennels. It was, said Dorothy Cleary, president of the local Animal Protection League, a "concentration camp for dogs."

As the years passed, the ranch became more like a canine nursing home. By 1973, only seventy dogs remained. By 1981, their number had shrunk to eight. They were moved to a private kennel and the ranch was sold. Musketeer, the last dog, finally succumbed in 1984.

Even with the expense of keeping the dogs and an out-of-court settlement in 1973 awarding $2 million to relatives of Ritchey's, the estate had grown to some $11 million by the time that Musketeer died. After his passing, the estate was handed over, as Ritchey had instructed, to Auburn University's school of veterinary medicine. □

The Hughes Legacy

Howard Hughes was a man in the grip of terrible obsessions. After flamboyant early years as a movie producer, playboy, and daredevil aviator, Hughes developed a lust for privacy so strong that he retreated from the world, seeing no one but a handful of aides.

Hughes was enormously rich and obsessed with preserving his wealth. He wrote and revised his will again and again. Nevertheless, when an emaciated and drug-addicted seventy-year-old Howard Hughes died in April of 1976, he left an estate estimated at one and a half billion dollars—and no valid will at all.

Even as a young man, Hughes was compulsive about his will. When he married for the first time, at the age of nineteen, he spent weeks drawing up the document. That will, and others that followed, directed that the bulk of his fortune be used for the Howard Hughes Medical Research Laboratories. In later years, he spent months writing and rewriting wills. But whenever he had a final draft, he found some reason to insert a new clause or delete an old one, forcing his personal secretary, Nadine Henley, to retype the entire document.

Hughes actually seems to have completed and signed two documents, in 1925 and 1938. But both were destroyed in favor of later efforts. In 1950, Hughes told Henley that he was once more ready to sign a document. She retrieved it from the bank and brought it to his bungalow at the Beverly Hills Hotel. Hughes studied the will closely, seeming to search for signs of tampering. Then he handed it back to

her—unsigned—and told her to return it to the safe-deposit box. And there it remained for the next quarter-century.

Hughes frequently assured the people around him that they would be remembered in his will. But the promises were always made in private, without witnesses. In his last year, as he lay near death, his aides tried desperately to determine where or whether a will existed. Hughes would ramble on, describing a document he had written in longhand while living in "the gray house," behind the tenth green of the Bel Air Country Club in Los Angeles. When pressed for details, however, the old man would snap, "You don't think I'm going to tell you where it is, do you?"

After Hughes's death, his aides

searched for the will in every place with any connection to the eccentric recluse—homes, hotels, banks, studios, company plants—but found no valid document. Meanwhile, independent of this effort, more than thirty wills surfaced on their own. The most famous purported to leave one-sixteenth of the estate to Melvin Dummar, a young truck driver who claimed to have given Hughes a ride when Hughes was hitchhiking in 1968.

None of the wills was honored, however. The government claimed more than 60 percent of the vast estate for inheritance taxes, and the balance of Hughes's money went to several relatives that the billionaire had shunned for years, one of whom he had—in one of his wills—specifically disinherited. □

Standing Room Only

Singer Kate Smith was a woman best known for heroic proportions—both in her imposing girth and in her powerful rendition of "God Bless America": Her stirring delivery of the song marked the opening of patriotic gatherings and athletic contests for decades, imbuing even the most lackluster event with grandeur. And so it seemed fitting that even in death Kate Smith occasioned a discussion of size—this involving the proper proportions for her tomb.

Smith died in June of 1986 at the age of seventy-nine. In her will she asked to be buried in the Catholic Cemetery of Saint Agnes in Lake Placid, New York, where she had summered for thirty-five years. She also specified that she was to be interred in a pink- or rose-colored granite mausoleum "sufficient to contain my remains alone." The cost of the mausoleum was to be paid out of the $300,000 that she left to Saint Agnes Church. But

what seemed to be a simple request led to a legal battle that lasted more than a year.

The problem was Saint Agnes had a policy against aboveground burial sites. The church did not even like large tombstones. So church officials cautiously offered to erect a "sarcophagus-type mausoleum," three feet ten inches high, four feet nine inches wide, and nine feet six inches long. "Three feet high is not a mausoleum," asserted one executor of the estate. Smith's sister Helena Steene insisted that "it has to be a walk-in, that's the difference," and proposed a building eleven feet high and nine feet four inches wide at a cost of $90,000.

Dickering over dimensions continued while Smith's body lay in a cold-storage vault. But finally the architect—Steene's son-in-law—and the churchmen reached a compromise: The mausoleum would be six feet eight inches high, seven feet seven inches wide, and ten feet

nine inches long. It would have a flat roof and cost $63,400. On November 14, 1987, with Smith finally entombed, the pastor of Saint Agnes blessed the mausoleum.

But some of the singer's many fans had already honored her. The month before her burial, on October 8, 1987, the Philadelphia Flyers hockey team dedicated a bronze statue of Smith at their arena. The team believed Smith brought them good luck every time they heard her version of "God Bless America," whether the performance was live or recorded. Not only did the Flyers act more expeditiously than Saint Agnes, they were not afraid of scale: The statue of Kate Smith stood some eight feet high and weighed more than a thousand pounds. □

The ashes of Oriole fan Elane Sollins were scattered around third base at Memorial Stadium *(right)*.

Sliding into Third

For almost thirty years, baseball fan Elane Sollins lived and breathed the Baltimore Orioles. She attended a score of the team's games each season, followed its fortunes on the radio, and watched nearly every game that was broadcast on television. Her favorite Oriole was third baseman Brooks Robinson, and her seat of choice was near him, along the third-base line. Sollins used to tell her family that when she died, she wanted her ashes scattered at third base in the Orioles' home park, Memorial Stadium.

After she died in October of 1988 at the age of sixty-three, Sollins got her wish. Baltimore's recreation department, which managed Memorial Stadium, cheerfully assented when Charles Kalus, Sollins's son, revealed his mother's request. Stadium manager Gordon Goetz helped Kalus find third base when he arrived with his mother's ashes—it was between seasons and the stadium's turf was torn up for repairs. Brooks Robinson, by then retired, confessed that he was flattered.

But three years later, Sollins's beloved Orioles deserted her. After thirty-seven years in Memorial Stadium, the team moved to a new home in downtown Baltimore. □

Pancho Villa, the hero of the Mexican revolution that began in 1910, was gunned down in Parral, Mexico, on June 20, 1923. As he lay dying, Villa groped unsuccessfully for meaningful last words. "Don't let it end like this," he reportedly begged his men. "Tell them I said something."

Bytes from Beyond

David Hughes takes his laptop computer everywhere—to the grocery store and his neighborhood bar in Colorado Springs, in the car, on airplane trips and horseback rides. He even plans to take it with him to the grave. A much-decorated retired army colonel and West Point graduate, Hughes has stipulated in his will that he wants to be buried with his latest laptop and state-of-the-art software that will enable him to go on-line after his death.

Across America, hundreds of thousands of computer aficionados exchange messages and hold round-table conversations, or "chats," over electronic networks. It is arguable that none is more enthusiastic than Hughes, who since 1981 has been owner of a computer bulletin board, the Old Colorado City Electronic Cottage. He calls computer networks "highways of the mind" and holds an almost mystical

Demonstrating the kind of facilities he wants available in his grave, David Hughes taps out a message on his portable computer, sending it to an electronic bulletin board via the modem and cordless telephone beside him.

conviction in their ability to convey information. In some way, he believes, the microchip in his computer is an extension of his mind. It can continue to grow, learn, think, and network, even after he dies.

The laptop designated in David Hughes's last testament as his in-ground companion will, he hopes, serve as his mouthpiece. Powered by a solar electric panel and linked by radio with computer networks throughout the world, it would, if Hughes's wishes come true, engage in digital dialogue with the living from the grave. Its opening gambit would be "Hi! This is Dave Hughes. Wanna chat?" □

Deep Pockets

The editors at *Forbes* magazine were thrashing out the details of a story when, suddenly, the sound of a roaring engine smothered their words. They ran to the window, but nothing was amiss outside. The source of the noise was near at hand—a motorcycle was racing down the hall, and astride it sat publisher Malcolm Forbes.

Forbes was a man with a gigantic appetite for living and, luckily, the wherewithal to sate it—he had built the magazine he inherited from his father into a veritable money machine. Forbes had so much wealth and so many acquisitions that his will ran to a remarkable sixty-one pages. The billionaire publisher was an unabashed consumer.

He owned no fewer than eight residences around the world, including a forty-seven-room château in France; a ranch in Colorado; a South Seas pied-à-terre on Laucala, his private island in Fiji; and a palace once home to the governor of Tangier. Forbes celebrated his seventieth and last birthday there in August 1989 with a two-million-dollar party whose lavishness prompted gossip columnists to wonder whether the birthday boy had perhaps exceeded the bounds of good taste.

Forbes cruised aboard his 151-foot yacht, traveled in a private Boeing 727 jet dubbed the *Capitalist Tool,* and floated aloft in the flagship of his hot-air balloon fleet. Seized in his later years by a fancy for motorcycles, the footloose

Combining twin passions of motorcycling and ballooning, billionaire publisher Malcolm Forbes *(above, in basket)* inflated a 187-foot balloon at his New Jersey estate in 1986. Wearing the colors of Forbes's own cycle club, a member *(left)* rides the publisher's real Harley-Davidson to his memorial service in March of 1990.

Forbes led packs of riders across China, Pakistan, Egypt, Thailand, Germany, and Turkey, with his balloons trailing overhead. He owned twelve jeweled Fabergé eggs—the largest such collection outside the Kremlin—and scores of paintings by great artists. At his command was a 5,000-man army composed entirely of tin soldiers.

In his voluminous will, Forbes seemed intent that the party go on without him. He left $1,000 to each of the proprietors of his nine favorite restaurants in New York City. More than two dozen motorcycle clubs received $1,000 bequests because, Forbes explained, their "Sunday runs provided so much pleasure and fellowship for me and so many other cycling enthusiasts." He also set aside $10,000 for the American Motorcyclist Association. Every employee at *Forbes* magazine received an extra week's salary, and all employee loans up to $10,000 were forgiven.

Forbes directed that he be cremated and his ashes buried on Laucala. The epitaph on his grave was to read, "WHILE ALIVE, HE LIVED." His instructions were carried out, as usual, to the letter. □

ACKNOWLEDGMENTS

The editors wish to thank these individuals and institutions for their valuable assistance:

Roger Ahlgrim, Ahlgrim & Sons, Palatine, Ill.; Joseph Albright, Alexandria, Va.; Amnesty International U.S.A., New York; Garry D. Aney, Town of Warren, Mohawk, N.Y.; Lawrence C. Anspach, American Cemetery/Mortuary Consultants, Chicago; Lois Archuleta, Salt Lake City Public Library, Salt Lake City; Jon Bekken, Champaign, Ill.; Betty T. Bennett, College of Arts and Sciences, American University, Washington, D.C.; Philip Bergen, Bostonian Society, Boston; Françoise Berthelot-Vinchon, Paris; Regis Braux, Bureau de la Conservation, Cimetière du Père-Lachaise, Paris; Burlington Public Library, Burlington, Colo.; Dick Cavett, New York; Chris Clemens, Lewisburg, Pa.; Ivan Colovic, Ethnographic Institute of the Serbian Academy of Science and Arts, Belgrade; Judith Curtis, Adams National Historic Site, Quincy, Mass.; Eddie Dean, *Potomac News*, Woodbridge, Va.; James M. Elson, Red Hill Patrick Henry Memorial, Brookneal, Va.; Enoch Pratt Library, Maryland Department, Baltimore; Michael R. Gannett, Cornwall Historical Society, Cornwall, Conn.; Alex Ghia, Ghia Gallery, San Francisco; Hans-Joachim Giersberg, Stiftung Schlösser und Gärten Potsdam-Sanssouci, Potsdam; John Graham, Cincinnati Historical Society, Cincinnati; Pamela Green, Erie County Historical Society, Erie, Pa.; Bruce Gurner, Gurner Photography, Water Valley, Miss.; Jack Gurner, Gurner Photography, Water Valley, Miss.; Mary L. Hartman, Princeton Public Library, Princeton, N.J.; David Hughes, Colorado Springs; Ilion Free Public Library, Ilion, N.Y.; Karl-Heinz Janssen, Die Zeit, Hamburg; Edward Johnson, Chicago; Gail Johnson, Chicago; Melissa Johnson, Chicago; Christopher Joyce, Annapolis; Charles Kalus, Baltimore; Norma Keeler, Burlington, Colo.; John Mark Lamberton, Kansas State Historical Society, Topeka; Anton LaVey, San Francisco; Leavenworth Public Library, Leavenworth, Kans.; Dick Levinson, National Museum of Health & Medicine, Washington, D.C.; Connie Lingle, University of Southern Mississippi, Hattiesburg; Pam Lundy, Will Rogers High School, Tulsa, Okla.; John R. Mathews, Washington, D.C.; Mara Miniati, Istituto e Museo di Storia della Scienza, Florence; Georg Minkenberg, Domkapitel, Aachen; Museum of Mourning Art, Meadowbrook, Pa.; Larz F. Neilson, *Town Crier*, Wilmington, Mass.; Guy Nichols, Fort Smith National Historic Site, Fort Smith, Ark.; Fred Olds, Guthrie, Okla.; Oneida County Historical Society, Utica, N.Y.; Kristin Onuf, Monticello, Charlottesville, Va.; Soeur Patricia, Monastère de la Visitation, Annecy, France; Otto E. Plettenbacher, Vienna; L. R. Poos, Catholic University of America, Washington, D.C.; Franca Principe, Istituto e Museo di Storia della Scienza, Florence; Richard R. Falk Associates, Public Relations Services, New York; Mi Mi Rivera, Urbana, Ill.; Suzanne M. Shultz, Polyclinic Medical Center, Harrisburg, Pa.; Mark Smith, Pittsburg; Jeff Stein, Urbana, Ill.; Jack Stephens, Alexander Graham Bell National Historic Site, Baddeck, Nova Scotia; Mark Tarallo, Washington, D.C.; Beverly Tetterton, New Hanover County Public Library, Wilmington, N.C.; Town of Warren Historical Association, Jordanville, N.Y.; Mireille de Vaumas, Versailles; Thomas Webber, Telophase Society, San Diego; Bernard Weiss, National Music Service Corporation, Spokane; Wilmington Memorial Library, Wilmington, Mass.; Gretchen Worden, Mutter Museum, Philadelphia; Jim Yardley, *Atlanta Journal-Constitution*, Marietta, Ga.; Stephen Zawistowski, A.S.P.C.A., Humane Education, New York.

PICTURE CREDITS

The sources for the illustrations that appear in this book are listed below. Credits from left to right are separated by semicolons, from top to bottom by dashes.

Cover: Archiv für Kunst und Geschichte, Berlin, background, Melvin J. Ingber/Photo Researchers Inc., New York. **3:** Archiv für Kunst und Geschichte, Berlin. **7:** Al Honig/Ghia Gallery, San Francisco, background, Kouichiro Shimauchi/Photonica, New York. **8:** Archiv für Kunst und Geschichte, Berlin—Dom Kapital Aachen, foto Münchow. **9:** UPI/Bettmann, New York. **10:** The Trustees of the Victoria and Albert Museum, London—Thierry Secretan. **11:** AP/Wide World Photos, New York, background, UPI/Bettmann, New York. **12:** From *Premature Burial and How It May be Prevented*, by William Tebb, F.R.G.S., and Colonel Edward Perry Vollum, M.D., Swan Sonnenschein and Co., Ltd., London, 1905. **13:** The William Morris Gallery, Walthamstow, London. **14:** Town of Warren Historical Association, Jordanville, N.Y. **15:** Carl Iwaski for *LIFE*. **16, 17:** Courtesy Time Inc. Magazines Picture Collection. **18:** Mark Smith, Venice. **19:** UPI/Bettmann, New York. **20:** AP/Wide World Photos, New York—Bettmann Newsphotos, New York. **21:** Al Honig/Ghia Gallery, San Francisco—Alden Lee Holsopple, Hayward, Calif. **22:** Jean-Loup Charmet, Paris. **23:** Museum of Mourning Art, Drexel Hill, Pa. **24, 25:** Luc Girard—Anatomic Museum, Leiden University, Leiden. **26:** Library of Congress LC 2011234. **27:** © 1991 Ted H. Hoffman. **28:** © 1989 Jon Blumb. **29:** © Gilles Perez/Magnum Photos, New York. **30:** Juan Sosa. **31:** Lawrence C. Anspach, courtesy Cedar Park Cemetery, Chicago. **32:** Imre Szabo, Belgrade. **33:** National Music Service Corporation, Spokane, line art by Time-Life Books. **34:** © Debra Lex. **35:** UPI/Bettmann, New York. **36:** *The Japan Times*, Toyko. **37:** Roger Ahlgrim. **38:** Art by Time-Life Books. **39:** Silkeborg Museum, Denmark, background, Roy Murphy/STIM/Photri, Inc., Falls Church, Va. **40, 41:** Mary Evans Picture Library, London; Department of Anatomy, University of Edinburgh, Edinburgh. **42:** Courtesy the Cincinnati Historical Society, Cincinnati, hand colored by Karen Doyle. **43:** Courtesy the National Museum of Health & Medicine, Washington, D.C. **44:** ASL Suisses, Lausanne—art by Time-Life Books. **45:** Michael Holford, London. **46:** Courtesy the Erie Historical Museum and Planetarium, Erie, Pa. **47:** The Bettmann Archive, New York. **48:** UPI/Bettmann, New York. **49:** Cacciapuoti/Nouvellepresse, Naples. **50:** Peter Clayton, Hemel Hempstead, England. **51:** Alinari, Florence, hand colored by Karen Doyle. **52:** Alinari, Florence. **53:** Western History Collections, University of Oklahoma, Norman. **54:** Courtesy Lincoln County Heritage Trust, Lincoln, N.Mex. **55:** From *The Saga of Sitting Bull's Bones*, by Robb DeWall, Korczak's Heritage, Inc., Crazy Horse, S.Dak., 1984, courtesy the Crazy Horse Memorial Archives, Crazy Horse, S.Dak. **56:** Silkeborg Museum, Denmark. **57:** Courtesy the National Museum of Natural History, Washington, D.C. **58:** Juana Anderson/*Philadelphia Daily News* Photo, Philadelphia. **59:** Roger Viollet, Paris—courtesy Walnut Street Theatre, Philadelphia. **60:** Enrico Martino/Team, Rome. **61:** Erich Lessing/Magnum Photos, Paris. **62:** Courtesy the Rhode Island Historical Society, Providence; Franca Principe, Florence, courtesy Istituto e Museo di Storia della Scienza, Florence. **63:** Doubleday, Doran. **64:** Malcolm Denmark, *Florida Today*, Melbourne—© 1977 *Star Tribune*, Minneapolis-St. Paul. **65:** From *A History of Wine in America from the Beginnings to Prohibition*, by Thomas Pinney, the Regents of the University of California, Berkeley Press, Los Angeles, 1989. **66:** Courtesy Summum, Salt Lake City. **67:** Samuel Psoras, courtesy Mutter Museum, College of Physicians of Philadelphia, Philadelphia, background, Robert Landau/Westlight, Los Angeles. **68:** Sanford H. Roth/Rapho-Guillumette, Photo Researchers, New York. **69:** The Bettmann Archive, New York. **70:** Mark Crosse/*Fresno Bee*, Fresno, Calif. **71:** Renee Comet. **72, 73:** *Boston Globe* Photo, Boston. **74:** Courtesy the Trustees of the British Library, London. **75:** Cliché Musée de L'Air et de L'Espace. **76:** Photo by J. E. France, from the Bruce Gurner Collection, Water Valley, Miss.—the Michael Ochs Archives, Venice, Calif. **77:** From *The Newgate Calender*, Vol. 11, Andrew Knapp and William Baldwin, 1825. **78, 79:** UPI/Bettmann, New York. **80:** Delft City Museum, Het Prinsenhof, Delft. **81:** The National Galleries of Scotland. **82:** National Portrait Gallery, London; Mary Evans Picture Library, London. **83:** Buffalo and Erie County Historical Society, Buffalo, N.Y. **84:** National Museum, Stockholm. **85:** Renee Comet (5)—Hart Crane Papers, Rare Books and Manuscripts Library, Columbia University, New York. **86:** AP/Wide World Photos, New York. **87:** Oroville Mercury Register/California State University, Meriam Library, Chico—Renee Comet. **88:** Richard McGuire for Noah's Ark Rehabilitation Center, Inc., Locust Grove, Ga. **89:** Courtesy the Cavalry and Guards Club, London. **90, 91:** Scala, Florence; UPI/Bettmann, New York, courtesy the University of Southern Mississippi, McCain Library and Archives, Hattiesburg. **92:** Courtesy the Yang family and O'Conner School Pictures, Tewksbury, R.I.—Sedge Le Blanq/OPERA NEWS, New York. **93:** Scala, Florence. **94:** Giraudon, Paris. **95:** Samuel Psoras, courtesy the Mutter Museum, College of Physicians of Philadelphia, Philadelphia; North Carolina Collection, University of North Carolina at Chapel Hill. **96, 97:** Renee Comet, courtesy Don Jurick for Will Rogers High School, Tulsa, Okla.—Co Rentmeester for *LIFE*; Rex Features, London. **98:** The Blood-Horse Collection, Lexington, Ky. **99:** Mary Evans Picture Library, London, background, Mark Stephenson/Westlight, Los Angeles. **100:** Yale University Art Gallery, New Haven, Conn. **101:** Bibliothèque Nationale, Paris—Henry Gros-

BIBLIOGRAPHY

Books

Allen, Reginald S. *W. S. Gilbert: An Anniversary Survey and Exhibition Checklist*. Charlottesville, Va.: Bibliographical Society of the University of Virginia, 1963.

Andrews, Deborah (Ed.). *The Annual Obituary 1989*. Chicago: St. James Press, 1990.

Asimov, Isaac. *Asimov's Biographical Encyclopedia of Science and Technology*. Garden City, N.Y.: Doubleday, 1982.

Baedeker's Moscow. Great Britain: Jarrold & Sons, 1987.

Bain, R. Nisbet. *Gustavus III: And His Contemporaries, 1746-1792*. London: Kegan Paul, Trench, Trübner, 1894.

Baker, Nina Brown. *William the Silent*. New York: Vanguard Press, 1947.

Barlett, Donald L., and James E. Steele. *Empire: The Life, Legend, and Madness of Howard Hughes*. New York: W. W. Norton, 1979.

Barozzi, Jacques. *Guide des Cimetières Parisiens*. Paris: Éditions Hervas, 1990.

Bayle, Pierre. *Dictionnaire Historique et Critique*. Rotterdam: M. Böhm, 1820 (reprint of 1720 edition).

Beath, Warren Newton. *The Death of James Dean*. New York: Grove Press, 1986.

Benton, Richard G. *Death and Dying*. New York: Van Nostrand Reinhold, 1978.

Bergheim, Laura. *Weird, Wonderful America*. New York: Collier Books, 1988.

Bernacchi, L. C. *A Very Gallant Gentleman*. London: Thornton Butterworth, 1933.

Biographie Universelle Ancienne et Moderne. Paris: Thoisnier Desplaces, 1843.

Blackington, Alton H. *Yankee Yarns*. New York: Dodd, Mead, 1954.

Boase, T. S. R. *Death in the Middle Ages*. New York: McGraw-Hill, 1972.

Bockris, Victor. *With William Burroughs: A Report from the Bunker*. New York: Seaver Books, 1981.

Brand, John. *Observations on the Popular Antiquities of Great Britain*. Detroit: Singing Tree Press, Book Tower, 1969.

Brandreth, Gyles:
Famous Last Words & Tombstone Humor. New York: Sterling, 1989.

The Last Word. New York: Sterling, 1979.

Brinkle, Lydle. *Hippocrene Companion Guide to the Soviet Union*. New York: Hippocrene Books, 1990.

Bushell, Peter. *Great Eccentrics*. London: George Allen & Unwin, 1984.

Byrne, Julia Clare. *Curiosities of the Search Room*. Detroit: Singing Tree Press, Book Tower, 1969 (reprint of 1880 edition).

Canby, Courtlandt. *A History of Flight* (Vol. 3). New York: Hawthorne Books, 1963.

Caufield, Catherine. *The Emperor of the United States of America & Other Magnificent British Eccentrics*. New York: St. Martin's Press, 1981.

Cavalier, Julian. *American Castles*. Cranberry, N.J.: A. S. Barnes, 1973.

Chappelow, Allan. *Shaw: "The Chucker-Out."* New York: AMS Press, 1971.

Clark, James M. *The Dance of Death: In the Middle Ages and the Renaissance*. Glasgow: Jackson, Son, 1950.

Clark, Ronald W. *The Life and Times*. New York: Avon Books, 1984.

Clemens, Christopher, and Mark Smith. *Death: Grim Realities and Comic Relief*. New York: Delacorte Press, 1982.

Coffin, Margaret M. *Death in Early America*. Nashville: Thomas Nelson, 1976.

Considine, Millie, and Ruth Pool. *Wills: A Dead Giveaway*. Garden City, N.Y.: Doubleday, 1974.

Crawford, Christina. *Mommie Dearest*. New York: William Morrow, 1978.

Cronholm, Neander N. *A History of Sweden* (Vol. 2). Chicago: Neander N. Cronholm, 1902.

Culbertson, Judi, and Tom Randall:
Permanent Californians. Chelsea, Vt.: Chelsea Green, 1989.

Permanent Parisians. Chelsea, Vt.: Chelsea Green, 1986.

Curl, James Stevens. *A Celebration of Death*. New York: Charles Scribner's Sons, 1980.

Cushing, Harvey. *The Life of Sir William Osler* (Vol. 1). Oxford: Clarendon Press, 1925.

Daily, Patrick. *Patrick Henry: The Last Years, 1789-1799*. Bedford, Va.: Descendants Branch—Patrick Henry Memorial Foundation, 1986.

Dakers, Andrew. *The Tragic Queen: A Study of Mary Queen of Scots*. London: Hutchinson, 1931.

Dark, Sidney, and Rowland Grey. *W. S. Gilbert: His Life and Letters*. London: Methuen, 1923.

Davey, Richard. *A History of Mourning*. London: McCorquodale, 1890.

Davidson, Angus. *Miss Douglas of New York*. New York: Viking Press, 1953.

Davis, H. W. C., and J. R. H. Weaver (Eds.). *The Dictionary of National Biography*. London: Oxford University Press, 1927.

Dedication of the Equestrian Statue of Major-General John Sedgwick. Hartford: State of Connecticut, 1913.

De La Laurence, Lionel. *Lully*. Paris: F. Alcan, 1911.

Desti, Mary. *The Untold Story: The Life of Isadora Duncan, 1921-1927*. New York: Da Capo Press, 1981.

DeWall, Robb. *The Saga of Sitting Bull's Bones*. Sioux Falls, S. Dak.: Modern Press, 1984.

Dickerson, Robert B., Jr. *Final Placement*. Algonac, Mich.: Reference Publications, 1982.

Dictionary of the Middle Ages (Vol. 10). New York: Charles Scribner's Sons, 1988.

Dictionnaire de Biographie Francaise. Paris: Librarie Letouzay et Ane, 1954.

Dos Passos, John. *The Portugal Story: Three Centuries of Exploration and Discovery*. Garden City, N.Y.: Doubleday, 1969.

Douglas, Hugh. *Burke and Hare*. London: Robert Hale, 1973.

Dowden, Edward. *The Life of Percy Bysshe Shelley*. New York: Barnes & Noble, 1966.

Eaton, Quaintance. *The Miracle of the Met*. New York: Meredith Press, 1968.

Ellman, Richard. *Oscar Wilde*. London: Hamish Hamilton, 1988.

Encyclopædia Britannica (Vol. 11). Chicago: Encyclopædia Britannica, 1960.

The Encyclopedia Americana (Vol. 13). Danbury, Conn.: Grolier, 1986.

Ervine, John. *Bernard Shaw: His Life, Work and Friends*. New York: William Morrow, 1956.

Facts and Fallacies. Pleasantville, N.Y.: Reader's Digest Association, 1988.

Facts On File Yearbook 1989. New York: Facts On File, 1990.

Forbes, Malcolm, and Jeff Bloch. *They Went That-a-Way . . . .* New York: Simon & Schuster, 1988.

Fradin, Dennis Brindell. *Patrick Henry: "Give Me Liberty or Give Me Death!"* Hillside, N.J.: Enslow, 1990.

Franklin, Joe. *Classics of the Silent Screen.* New York: Citadel Press, 1959.

Fraser, Antonia. *Mary, Queen of Scots.* New York: Delacorte Press, 1969.

Gaddis, Thomas E., and James O. Long. *Killer: A Journal of Murder.* New York: Macmillan, 1970.

Gallaudet Encyclopedia of Deaf People and Deafness (Vol. 1). New York: McGraw-Hill, 1987.

Garrison, Webb. *Strange Facts about Death.* Abingdon: Parthenon Press, 1978.

Gillispie, Charles Coulston (Ed.). *Dictionary of Scientific Biography* (Vols. 3 & 12). New York: Charles Scribner's Sons, 1975, 1980.

Gittings, Clare. *Death, Burial and the Individual in Early Modern England.* London: Croom Helm, 1984.

Glob, P. V. *The Bog People.* Translated by Rupert Bruce-Mitford. Ithaca, N.Y.: Cornell University Press, 1969.

Gould, Lewis L. *The Presidency of William McKinley.* Lawrence: Regents Press of Kansas, 1980.

Green, A. Wigfall. *The Man Bilbo.* Baton Rouge: Louisiana State University Press, 1963.

Grundy, Milton. *Venice Recorded.* London: Angus & Robertson, 1971.

Habenstein, Robert W., and William M. Lamers. *The History of American Funeral Directing* (2nd rev. ed.). Milwaukee, Wis.: National Funeral Directors, 1985.

Haile, Martin. *Life of Reginald Pole* (2nd ed.). London: Sir Isaac Pitman & Sons, 1911.

Harris, Virgil M. *Ancient, Curious and Famous Wills.* Boston: Little, Brown, 1911.

Harrison, Frederic. *William the Silent.* New York: Charles Scribner's Sons, 1924.

Hart-Davis, Rupert (Ed.). *The Letters of Oscar Wilde.* New York: Harcourt, Brace & World, 1962.

Hastings, James (Ed.). *Encyclopædia of Religion and Ethics* (Vol. 11). Edinburgh: T. & T. Clark, 1920.

Heer, Friedrich. *Charlemagne and His World.* New York: Macmillan, 1975.

Hellman, Lillian. *Pentimento: A Book of Portraits.* Boston: Little, Brown, 1973.

Hendin, David. *Death as a Fact of Life.* New York: W. W. Norton, 1973.

Honour, Hugh. *The Companion Guide to Venice.* London: Collins, 1965.

Hoskins, Robert. *Louis Armstrong: Biography of a Musician.* Los Angeles: Holloway House, 1979.

Howlett, John. *James Dean: A Biography.* New York: Simon & Schuster, Fireside Book, 1975.

Hunter, Kay. *Duet for a Lifetime.* New York: Coward-McCann, 1964.

Israel, Lee. *Miss Tallulah Bankhead.* New York: G. P. Putnam's Sons, 1972.

Jaynes, Gregory, and the Editors of Time-Life Books. *The Killing Ground: Wilderness to Cold Harbor* (The Civil War series). Alexandria, Va.: Time-Life Books, 1986.

Johns, A. Wesley. *The Man Who Shot McKinley.* South Brunswick: A. S. Barnes, 1970.

Johnson, Allen (Ed.). *Dictionary Of American Biography* (Vol. 1). New York: Charles Scribner's Sons, 1936.

Johnson, Marion. *The Borgias.* London: Book Club, 1981.

Jones, Arthur. *Malcolm Forbes: Peripatetic Millionaire.* New York: Harper & Row, 1977.

Jones, Barbara. *Design for Death.* Indianapolis: Bobbs-Merrill, 1967.

Joyce, Christopher, and Eric Stover. *Witnesses from the Grave: The Stories Bones Tell.* Boston: Little, Brown, 1991.

Jullian, Philippe. *Oscar Wilde.* Translated by Violet Wyndham. London: Constable, 1969.

Kastenbaum, Robert, and Beatrice Kastenbaum (Eds.). *Encyclopedia of Death.* Phoenix: Oryx Press, 1989.

Katz, Ephraim. *The Film Encyclopedia.* New York: Thomas Y. Crowell, 1979.

Keisling, William, and Richard Kearns. *The Sins of Our Fathers.* Harrisburg, Pa.: William Keisling & Richard Kearns, 1988.

Kly, Y. N. (Ed.). *The Black Book: The True Political Philosophy of Malcolm X (El Hajj Malik El Shabazz).* Atlanta: Clarity Press, 1986.

Knapp, Andrew, and William Baldwin. *The Newgate Calendar* (Vol. 2). London: J. Robins, 1825.

Kurella, Hans. *Cesare Lombroso: A Modern Man of Science.* Translated by M. Eden Paul. London: Rebman, 1911.

Lamb, Harold. *Charlemagne: The Legend and the Man.* Garden City, N.Y.: Doubleday, 1954.

Langlade, Vincent de. *History of Père-Lachaise.* Conde-sur-Noireau: Éditions Vermet, 1988.

Limb, Sue, and Patrick Cordingley. *Captain Oates: Soldier and Explorer.* London: B. T. Batsford, 1982.

Livermore, H. V. *A New History of Portugal* (2nd ed.). Cambridge: Cambridge University Press, 1976.

Lockyer, Herbert. *Last Words of Saints and Sinners.* Grand Rapids, Mich.: Kregel, 1969.

Macdougall, Allan Ross. *Isadora: A Revolutionary in Art and Love.* New York: Thomas Nelson & Sons, 1960 .

Mailer, Norman. *The Executioner's Song.* Boston: Little, Brown, 1979.

Malcolm X. *The Autobiography of Malcolm X.* New York: Ballantine Books, 1973.

Mann, May. *Jayne Mansfield: A Biography.* London: Abelard-Schuman, 1973.

Marion, John Francis. *Famous and Curious Cemeteries.* New York: Crown Publishers, 1977.

Marsh, Clifton E. *From Black Muslims to Muslims: The Transition from Separatism to Islam, 1930-1980.* Metuchen, N.J.: Scarecrow Press, 1984.

Marvin, Frederic Rowland. *The Last Words of Distinguished Men and Women.* New York: Fleming H. Revell, 1901.

Mathew, Arnold H. *The Life and Times of Rodrigo Borgia: Pope Alexander VI.* London: Stanley Paul, 1912.

Mayer, Robert G. *Embalming History, Theory, and Practice.* Norwalk, Conn.: Appleton & Lange, 1990.

Mee, Charles L., Jr. *White Robe, Black Robe.* New York: G. P. Putnam's Sons, 1972.

Menchin, Robert S.:
The Last Caprice. New York: Simon & Schuster, 1963.

Where There's a Will. New York: Farnsworth, 1979.

Miall, Agnes. *William the Silent.* London: George G. Harrap, 1914.

Mitford, Jessica. *The American Way of Death.* New York: Simon & Schuster, 1963.

Moncrif, Paradis de. *Dissertation sur la Preminences des Chats dans la Société.* Rotterdam: J. D. Beman, 1741.

Morgan, Chester M. *Redneck Liberal: Theodore G. Bilbo and the New Deal.* Baton Rouge: Louisiana State University Press, 1985.

Morgan, Ted. *Literary Outlaw: The Life and Times of William S. Burroughs.* New York: Henry Holt, 1988.

Nash, Jay Robert. *Look for the Woman.* New York: M. Evans, 1981.

Nass, Herbert E. *Wills of the Rich and Famous.* New York: Warner Books, 1991.

The New Encyclopædia Britannica (Vols. 3, 6, & 15). Chicago: Encyclopædia Britannica, 1984, 1985, 1988.

Newman, Joyce. *Jean-Baptiste de Lully and His Tragédies Lyriques.* Ann Arbor: University of Michigan Research Press, 1979.

Newquist, Roy. *Conversations with Joan Crawford.* Secaucus, N.J.: Citadel Press, 1980.

Notable American Women, 1607-1950: A Biographical Dictionary (Vol. 1). Boston: Radcliffe College, 1971.

Olcott, Charles S. *The Life of William McKinley* (Vol. 2). Boston: Houghton Mifflin, 1916.

Orkin, Mark M. *The Great Stork Derby.* Don Mills, Ontario: General Publishing, 1981.

Ovsianikov, Yuri. *Invitation to Russia.* New York: Rizzoli, 1989.

Panati, Charles. *Panati's Extraordinary Endings of Practically Everything and Everybody.* New York: Harper & Row, 1989.

Parrish, Roy Gibson. "Death in the Night: Mysterious Syndrome in Asian Refugees." In *Medical and Health Annual,* edited by Ellen Bernstein. Chicago: Encyclopædia Britannica, 1984.

Parry, Edward. *The Persecution of Mary Stewart.* New York: Charles Scribner's Sons, 1931.

Pearson, Hesketh:
Gilbert: His Life and Strife. New York: Harper & Brothers, 1957.

Gilbert and Sullivan: A Biography. London: MacDonald & Jane's, 1975.

The Penguin Concise Dictionary of Biographical Quotation. New York: Penguin Books, 1978.

Picard, Barbara Leonie. *The Tower & the Traitors.* New York: G. P. Putnam's Sons, 1961.

Platt, John, Chris Dreja, and Jim McCarty. *Yardbirds.* London: Sidgwick & Jackson, 1983.

Puckle, Bertram S. *Funeral Customs: Their Origin and Development.* London: T. Werner Laurie, 1926.

Putnam, Ruth. *William the Silent: Prince of Orange, 1533-1584.* New York: G. P. Putnam's Sons, 1911.

Quincy, Thomas de. *Autobiographic Sketches* (Vol. 2). London: James Hogg & Sons, 1853.

Quiri, Patricia Ryon. *Alexander Graham Bell.* New York: Franklin Watts, 1991.

Rolling Stone Rock Almanac. New York: Rolling Stone Press Book, 1983.

Rolt, L. T. C. *The Aeronauts: A History of Ballooning, 1783-1903.* New York: Walker, 1966.

Roo, Peter de. *Material for a History of Pope Alexander VI: His Relatives and His Time* (Vol. 5). New York: Universal Knowledge Foundation, 1924.

Roscoe, William. *The Life and Pontificate of Leo the Tenth* (Vol. 2, 4th ed.). London: Henry G. Bohn, 1846.

Ross, Ishbel. *Charmers and Cranks: Twelve Famous American Women Who Defied the Conventions.* New York: Harper & Row, 1965.

Sadie, Stanley (Ed.). *The New Grove Dictionary of Music and Musicians* (Vol. 4). London: Macmillan, 1980.

Salter, Cedric. *Algarve and Southern Portugal.* New York: Hastings House, 1974.

Salter, J. T. (Ed.). *Public Men in and out of Office.* Chapel Hill: University of North Carolina Press, 1946.

Sann, Paul:
  Fads, Follies and Delusions of the American People. New York: Bonanza Books, 1967.
  The 20's: The Lawless Decade. New York: Crown, 1957.

Saxon, A. H. *P. T. Barnum: The Legend and the Man.* New York: Columbia University Press, 1989.

Sayen, Jamie. *Einstein in America: The Scientist's Conscience in the Age of Hitler and Hiroshima.* New York: Crown, 1985.

Schenk, W. *Reginald Pole: Cardinal of England.* London: Longmans, Green, 1950.

Scott, Maxwell Mrs. *The Tragedy at Fotheringay.* London: Adam & Charles Black, 1895.

Scott, R. H. F. *Jean-Baptiste Lully.* London: Peter Owen, 1973.

Semler, Helen Boldyreff. *Discovering Moscow.* New York: St. Martin's Press, 1989.

Shepherd, C. W. *Snuff: Yesterday and Today.* London: G. Smith & Sons, 1963.

Shepherd, Jack. *The Adams Chronicles: Four Generations of Greatness.* Boston: Little, Brown, 1975.

Shultz, Suzanne M. *Body Snatching: The Robbing of Graves for the Education of Physicians in Early Nineteenth Century America.* Jefferson, N.C.: McFarland, 1992.

Sicherman, Barbara, et al. (Eds.). *Notable American Women: The Modern Period.* Cambridge, Mass.: Harvard University Press, Belknap Press, 1980.

Sievers, Harry J. *Benjamin Harrison: Hoosier Statesman.* New York: University Publishers, 1959.

Sifakis, Carl. *The Encyclopedia of American Crime.* New York: Facts On File, 1982.

Silverman, Stephen M. *Where There's a Will . . . .* New York: Harper-Collins, 1991.

The Simon and Schuster Book of the Opera. New York: Simon & Schuster, 1977.

Slater, Scott, and Alec Solomita. *Exits.* New York: E. P. Dutton, 1980.

Smith, Desmond. *Smith's Moscow.* New York: Alfred A. Knopf, 1974.

Smith, Gibbs M. *Joe Hill.* Salt Lake City: University of Utah Press, 1969.

Smith, Page. *John Adams* (Vol. 2). Garden City, N.Y.: Doubleday, 1962.

Smoker, Barbara. "Man of Letters." In *The Genius of Shaw,* edited by Michael Holroyd. New York: Holt, Rinehart & Winston, 1979.

Spears, Monroe K. *Hart Crane.* Minneapolis: University of Minnesota Press, 1965.

Squire, Jack Collings. *William the Silent.* London: Methuen, 1912.

Stegner, Wallace. *Joe Hill.* New York: Penguin Books, 1990.

Stephen, Leslie, and Sidney Lee (Eds.). *The Dictionary of National Biography* (Vol. 16). London: Oxford University Press, 1917.

Stevens, Leslie C. *Russian Assignment.* Boston: Little, Brown, 1953.

Strait, Raymond. *The Tragic Secret Life of Jayne Mansfield.* Chicago: Henry Regnery, 1974.

Tebb, William, Edward Perry Vollum, and Walter R. Hadwen. *Premature Burial: And How It May Be Prevented.* London: Swan Sonnenschein, 1905.

Thomas, Bob. *Joan Crawford.* New York: Simon & Schuster, 1978.

Thomas, Frank. *Last Will and Testament.* New York: St. Martin's Press, 1972.

Truitt, Evelyn Mack. *Who Was Who on Screen.* New York: R. R. Bowker, 1984.

Tunstall, James. *Rambles about Bath and Its Neighborhood* (4th ed.). England: R. E. Peach, 1856.

Tytell, John. *Naked Angels: The Lives & Literature of the Beat Generation.* New York: McGraw-Hill, 1976.

Unterecker, John. *Voyager: A Life of Hart Crane.* New York: Farrar, Straus & Giroux, 1969.

Vaughan, Herbert M. *The Medici Popes: Leo X and Clement VII.* Port Washington, N.Y.: Kennikat Press, 1971 (reprint of 1908 edition).

Vogel, Susan, and Ima Ebong. *Africa Explores: 20th Century African Art.* New York: Center for African Art, 1991.

Wallace, Amy, David Wallechinsky, and Irving Wallace. *The Book of Lists #3.* New York: William Morrow, 1983.

Wallace, Irving, and Amy Wallace. *The Two.* New York: Simon & Schuster, 1978.

Wallace, Irving, David Wallechinsky, and Amy Wallace. *Significa.* New York: E. P. Dutton, 1983.

Wallechinsky, David, and Irving Wallace:
  The People's Almanac. Garden City, N.Y.: Doubleday, 1975.
  The People's Almanac #2. New York: William Morrow, 1978.
  The People's Almanac #3. Toronto: Bantam Books, 1981.

Warner, Gerald. *Being of Sound Mind.* London: Elm Tree Books, 1980.

Weber, Brom (Ed.). *The Complete Poems and Selected Letters and Prose of Hart Crane.* Garden City, N.Y.: Doubleday, Anchor Books, 1966.

Webster's New Biographical Dictionary. Springfield, Mass.: Merriam-Webster, 1988.

White, Trentwell Mason, and Ivan Sandrof. "The First Embalmer." In *Death: Grim Realities and Comic Relief,* edited by Christopher Clemens. New York: Delacorte Press, 1982.

Who Was Who in America (Vol. 1). Chicago: Marquis, 1968.

Willison, George F. *Patrick Henry and His World.* Garden City, N.Y.: Doubleday, 1969.

Wilson, Colin, and Donald Seaman. *The Encyclopedia of Modern Murder.* New York: Arlington House, 1988.

Winans, Christopher. *Malcolm Forbes: The Man Who Had Everything.* New York: St. Martins Press, 1990.

Winslow, Forbes. *The Anatomy of Suicide.* London: Henry, Renshaw, 1840.

Winslow, Richard Elliot, III. *General John Sedgwick: The Story of a Union Corps Commander.* Novato, Calif.: Presidio Press, 1982.

Wolfenstein, Eugene Victor. *The Victims of Democracy.* London: Free Association Books, 1989.

Periodicals

"Actor Leaves Legacy of Free Shoes." *American Funeral Director,* July 1984.

"After Gilmore, Who's Next to Die?" *Time,* January 31, 1977.

"After the General's Leg." *Time,* November 23, 1962.

"All Jazz Lovers Invited to Memorial for Satchmo." *Times-Picayune,* July 8, 1971.

Alsop, Joseph, and Stewart Alsop. "Lament for a Long-Gone Past." *Saturday Evening Post,* January 26, 1957.

"America's Songstress, Lake Placid's Friend, Kate Smith Passes Away." *Lake Placid News,* June 19, 1986.

Andrews, Robert M. "A Treasure Trove for Medical History Buffs." *Washington Post,* July 23, 1991.

Atkins, Martha. "Here's How You Can Become a Mummy." *Weekly World News,* February 13, 1990.

"Auburn to Get Over $18 Million." *Opelika Auburn-News,* August 28, 1972.

Avery, Ron. "They Put Their Brains to Work." *Philadelphia Daily News,* April 3, 1991.

"Baltimore Life: People, Pets and Eternal Rest." *Baltimore Magazine,* June 1979.

Baron, Roy C., et al. "Sudden Death among Southeast Asian Refugees." *Journal of the American Medical Association,* December 2, 1983.

Barry, Dave. "Watch Out for Identified Flying Objects, Especially Fish!" *Chicago Tribune,* October 4, 1987.

Batchelor, Jon. "To Heaven with Style." *SOMA,* Fall 1990.

Beal, Bruce. "Was She Eccentric in Life as in Death?" *San Antonio Light,* April 23, 1977.

Bearshaw, Brian. "Haunting Story of Miss Beswick's Mummy." *Manchester Evening News,* February 11, 1967.

"Beloved Pets Rest in Peace." *Baltimore Sun,* January 28, 1953.

Bennett, D. L.:
  "Billy Goat Kills Man." *Cherokee Tribune,* May 19, 1991.
  "Noah's Ark Harbors Infamous Killer Goat." *Cherokee Tribune,* May 26, 1991.

"The Beswick Family and the 'Manchester Mummy.' " *Manchester Weekly Times,* August 22, 1890.

"Bilbo Dead at 69 of Heart Ailment." *New York Times,* August 22, 1947.

Bishop, Edward Allen. "Casey Jones Legend Lives for 70 Years." *Clarion-Ledger Jackson Daily News,* April 19, 1970.

Blankman, Peter. "Spectral Crugar Mansion Awakening as Gelston Castle." *Utica Observer-Dispatch,* August 21, 1966.

Bluthardt, Robert T. "Wave of Death." *Firehouse,* June 1983.

Bolton, Amelia. "Auburn to Get Leftovers from Canine

Heirs." *Auburn Plainsman,* September 28, 1972.

Brackman, Barbara:

"Enchanted Kingdoms." *Americana,* August 1991.

"One Man's Eden." *Fine Homebuilding,* June-July 1991.

Brooks, Geraldine, and Tony Horwitz. "Iranians Mount Frenzied Farewell to Islamic Revolutionary Leader." *Wall Street Journal,* June 7, 1989.

Brotman, Barbara:

"7,000 Say Farewell to Flukey." *Chicago Tribune,* November 22, 1986.

"Under All the Trappings There Lies a Dope Dealer." *Chicago Tribune,* November 23, 1986.

Brown, Burtis S. "Details of the Failure of a 90-Foot Molasses Tank." *Engineering News-Record,* May 15, 1919.

Bruskin, Robert. "Senator Bilbo Dead at 69; White Supremacy Advocate." *Washington Post,* August 22, 1947.

Budd, James. "Killer Goat Gets Support." *Cherokee Citizen,* May 22, 1991.

Butler, Stacey. "Final Tribute to Man's Best Friend." *Baltimore Business Journal,* July 30-August 5, 1990.

"Cadillac Funeral." *American Funeral Director,* April 1984.

Campbell, Richard. "65-Year 'Run' about to End in Rest." *Los Angeles Herald Examiner,* December 19, 1976.

"Car Burial Rites Complete." *San Antonio Light,* May 19, 1977.

"Carl Panzran to His Death Early Friday Morning." *Leavenworth Times,* September 4, 1930.

Carlson, Peter, et al. "On the Road Again." *People,* June 16, 1986.

"Casey's Ride into History Has 73rd Birthday Today." *Commercial Appeal* (Memphis), April 30, 1973.

"Casket Carver." *LIFE,* June 6, 1988.

Chapin, Howard M. "Odd Phases of Rhode Island History." *Rhode Island Historical Society,* July 6, 1924.

"Charge against Kogut Awaits Outcome of Coroner's Inquest; Witness Overhears Liquor Deal." *Mercury-Register* (Oroville, Calif.), May 31, 1930.

"Charles Millar Dies Suddenly at Office." *Toronto Daily Star,* November 1, 1926.

"Charlie Chaplin's Body Vanishes from Grave." *Times,* March 3, 1978.

Chawkins, Steve. "David R. Hughes: Old Soldiers Never Die; They Just Keep Logging on." *Sunday Magazine Rocky Mountain News,* December 14, 1986.

"Chicago Gambler Buried in Cadillac-Style Coffin." *Jet,* March 19, 1984.

"Chicago's Flukey Stokes Met Same Tragic End as His Son." *Jet,* December 8, 1986.

"Coffin Stunt Kills Escapist." *Washington Times,* November 2, 1990.

Collingwood, Harris (Ed.). "May You Putt in Peace." *Business Week,* August 5, 1991.

"Compromise Quiets Haggling over Kate Smith's Mausoleum." *Lake Placid News,* August 6, 1987.

"Computer Fan Wants Post-Mortem Chats." *American Funeral Director,* December 1984.

Conrad, Barnaby, III. "The Best Address in Town." *Geo,* September 1984.

Cook, Bruce. "Forest Lawn Is More than Just a Ceme-

tery, It's a Repository of Art." *Chicago Tribune,* October 26, 1986.

Corelli, Rae, et al. "Grief and Frenzy." *Maclean's,* June 19, 1989.

"Coroner's Findings on Death in Dishwasher." *San Francisco Chronicle,* May 18, 1984.

Cory, Christopher T. "Journalists' Oriental Nightmare." *Psychology Today,* August 1981.

Costanzo, Joe, and Hal Knight. "Gary Mark Gilmore Dies before Utah Firing Squad." *Deseret News,* January 17, 1977.

Cotton, Gordon. "Casey's Legend Still Lives." *Yazoo City Herald,* July 22, 1973.

"A Course They're Just Dying to Play." *Golf Digest,* April 1991.

Cross, David. "Where Legends Lie." *Adirondack Life,* September-October 1991.

"Crowds Still Try to View Valentino." *New York Times,* August 27, 1926.

Cusick, Frederick:

"Dwyer Filled Speech with Accusations." *Philadelphia Inquirer,* January 25, 1987.

"Puzzling Behavior, and Then a Gunshot." *Philadelphia Inquirer,* January 23, 1987.

Cusick, Frederick, Dan Meyers, and Walter F. Roche, Jr. "Treasurer Dwyer Kills Self; Suicide at News Session." *Philadelphia Inquirer,* January 23, 1987.

"The Dead Smothered." *Boston Daily Globe,* January 16, 1919.

"Death and Devastation in Wake of North End Disaster." *Boston Daily Globe,* January 16, 1919.

"Death and Transfiguration." *Time,* March 5, 1965.

"Death for Kogut." *Mercury-Register* (Oroville, Calif.), June 12, 1930.

"Death of a Genius." *Time,* May 2, 1955.

"Death of Engineer Lahey." *Boston Post,* January 16, 1919.

"Deliveryman Crushed to Death." *Tampa Tribune,* May 9, 1991.

Dickens, Charles (Ed.). "Wills: Old and New." *All the Year Round,* August 23, 1890.

"Director at Will Rogers Dies at Spring Concert." *Tulsa Tribune,* April 24, 1974.

"Director Stricken at Concert, Dies." *Tulsa World,* April 24, 1974.

"Dog's Death Benefits Veterinary School." *American Funeral Director,* December 1984.

"Dog's Life: 81 Stray Canines Inherit Estate of Mistress Worth $14 Million." *New Kensington-Tarentum,* August 29, 1972.

Dold, R. Bruce. "A Funeral Parlor Puts Wakes in the Fast Lane." *Chicago Tribune,* October 12, 1989.

Draheim, H. Paul. "Picturesque Mansion Finest Mohawk Valley Landmark." *Evening Telegraph,* November 22, 1925.

"Dr. Hiller at Rest." *Boston Globe,* November 12, 1888.

"Drive-Up Funeral Home Gaining Acceptance." *New York Times,* January 31, 1977.

Dunlap, Mark. "Panzran Stalks to Death with Curse for All." *Topeka Capital,* September 6, 1930.

Dyer, Braven. "The Sports Parade." *Los Angeles Times,* February 7, 1947.

"Elkridge Cemetery Lets Pets, Owners Be 'Forever Together.' " *Baltimore Sun,* August 12, 1985.

Elliott, Carolyn. "Calm Gravesite—Sandra West." *San Antonio Light,* August 27, 1978.

Engel, Allison, and Margaret Engel. "The L. L. Been Catalogue." *Esquire,* November 1990.

Erlanger, Stephen. " 'Nightmare Death' Fells Thais, and Nations Bicker." *New York Times,* May 8, 1990.

"Estate Left for Library." *Semi-Weekly Sentinel* (Le Mars, Iowa), September 19, 1930.

Everett, Arthur. "Greats of Show Business Attend at Little Church." *Times-Picayune,* July 10, 1971.

Farquhar, Michael. "Remains to Be Seen." *Washington Post,* June 30, 1991.

Feeney, Joe, and Rebecca Johnston. "Sympathy for Snowball Melts the Urge to Kill." *Cherokee Tribune,* May 22, 1991.

"Ferrari Burial Okayed." *San Antonio Light,* April 12, 1977.

Ferrick, Thomas, Jr. "Years of Success Shadowed by Scandal." *Philadelphia Inquirer,* January 23, 1987.

"Finis for Petticoat Will Case." *Los Angeles Times,* May 12, 1927.

Fisher, Martin. "Frederick: The Grave." *Washington Post,* August 16, 1991.

"Fore!" *National Examiner,* March 12, 1991.

"Forever Stylish Drug Dealer Flukey Stokes Goes Out with a Bang." *People,* December 8, 1986.

"For Kate Smith, Death Alone Isn't Grounds for Burial." *People,* June 15, 1987.

"For Those in a Rush: Drive-Through Funerals." *American Funeral Director,* April 1989.

"Four Millar Winners Receive $100,000 Each; $25,000 Settles Suit." *Toronto Daily Star,* November 31, 1938.

"Fragment du Testament de Mademoiselle du Puy, Célèbre Joueuse de Harpe." *Le Mercure Galant,* December 1677.

Fredricksen, Barbara L. "Pets Preserved for Display: Costly Process Freeze-Dries Pets So They Last Indefinitely." *St. Petersburg Times,* January 6, 1987.

Frye, Ralph. "The Great Molasses Flood." *Reader's Digest,* August 1955.

"Funeral Awaits a Ruling." *San Antonio Light,* March 27, 1977.

Garland, Phyl. "Taps for Satchmo." *Ebony,* September 1971.

Gasior, Anne Burris. "Death Be Not Dull." *Daily Herald,* August 16, 1990.

Gilmore, Mikal. "Family Album." *Granta,* Autumn 1991.

Glosson, Ed, and Dave Manley. " 'Ferrari Funeral' Completed." *San Antonio Light,* May 19, 1977.

"A Goodies Way to Go—Laughing." *Eastern Daily Press* (Norwich, England), March 29, 1975.

Gordon, Rachel. "Unique Art Gallery Is at Death's Door." *San Francisco Independent,* April 3, 1990.

Gorner, Peter. "Lincoln's Genes May Help Reshape History." *Chicago Tribune,* February 17, 1991.

"Great Moments in Productivity." *Fortune,* September 1, 1986.

Greene, Bob:

"For 'Wimp,' the Cadillac of Funerals." *Chicago Tribune,* March 5, 1984.

"Next Up: 'Warning: I Brake for Funerals.' " *Chicago Tribune,* January 25, 1987.

Greene, Wade. "Guru of the Organic Food Cult." *New York Times,* June 6, 1971.

Grinnan, Edward. "Frigid Pet Tricks." *Seventeen,* July 1989.

Gurner, Jack, and Jessie Gurner. "Tales from the Rails." *Mississippi,* November-December 1989.

Gutman, John. "Leonard Warren." *Opera News,* April 2, 1960.

Haitch, Richard. "Drive-Up Funeral." *New York Times,* April 17, 1977.

Hamill, Pete. "Rodale, Food Guru, Dies at TV Taping." *New York Post,* June 8, 1971.

"Hanging Aug. 22." *Mercury-Register* (Oroville, Calif.), June 17, 1930.

Hannah, Dogen. "Controversial Exhibit: Artistic Side of Funerals." *Senior Spectrum,* September 1990.

Hart, J. "Elder North End Residents Recall the Molasses Flood of 1919." *Boston Tab,* January 12, 1988.

"Hazeltine Will Attacked." *Los Angeles Times,* May 26, 1925.

Herwig, Carol. "Orioles Fan's Odd Request: Scatter My Ashes on Third." *USA Today,* November 8, 1988.

Hewitt, Brian. " 'Catacombs' of Funeral Home a Mini Course." *Chicago Sun-Times,* March 8, 1991.

Hirsch, Ben. "Miniature Golf to Die For." *Inside Chicago,* January-February 1991.

"History for Sale." *Manchester Evening News,* June 15, 1972.

"Hollywood's Once and Only Star." *Time,* May 23, 1977.

Howell, Debi. "As the Urn Turns." *The City,* October 1990.

"Huge Molasses Tank Explodes in North End; 11 Dead, 50 Hurt." *Boston Post,* January 16, 1919.

"Husband Died of Laughing as He Watched TV." *Times* (London), March 29, 1975.

Jenkins, Jim:
 "Families: Ancestors Ordinary." *Greensboro Daily News,* April 30, 1978.
 "The Two." *Greensboro Daily News,* April 30, 1978.

"Jim Gernhart's Last Funeral." *Burlington Record,* January 24, 1980.

"J. I. Rodale Dead: Organic Farmer." *New York Times,* June 8, 1971.

Johnson, Edward C., Gail R. Johnson, and Melissa Johnson. "Mr. Thomas Holmes: The *True* Life and Career of the Pioneer Embalmer." *American Funeral Director* (Parts 1 & 2). July-August 1984.

Johnson, Robert. "After the Good Life, What Better Death than as a Mummy?" *Wall Street Journal,* October 28, 1988.

Jones, Rachel L., and Paul L. McGorrian. "The Memorable and the Madcap in North Pinellas County." *St. Petersburg Times,* January 1, 1988.

Jordan, Pat. "Freeze-Dried Memories." *Time,* February 13, 1989.

"Jury to Get Case Today; Defendant Declares He Bought Drinks at Rooms." *Mercury-Register* (Oroville, Calif.), June 13, 1930.

Kifner, John. "Final Tirade Heard as Throngs Mourn Khomeini." *New York Times,* June 6, 1989.

"Killer Goat Snowball Wins Reprieve from the Freezer." *Du Quoin (IL) Evening Call,* May 22, 1991.

Kirschner, Robert H., Friedrich A. O. Eckner, and Roy C. Baron. "The Cardiac Pathology of Sudden, Unexplained Nocturnal Death in Southeast Asian Refugees." *JAMA,* November 21, 1986.

Klinger, Rafael. "Going in Style. *XS,* August 7, 1991.

"Kogut Dies of Bomb Wounds." *Mercury-Register*

(Oroville, Calif.), October 20, 1930.

"Kogut Must Hang." *Mercury-Register* (Oroville, Calif.), June 14, 1930.

"Kogut's Last Words." *Mercury-Register* (Oroville, Calif.), October 21, 1930.

Kohlman, Matt. "Sitting Bull's Homecoming." *South Dakota Magazine,* March-April 1988.

Kurkjian, Tim. "For This O's Fan, It's Ashes to Ashes, Dust to 3rd Base." *Sun* (Baltimore), November 7, 1988.

Kuzniak, Russ. "Harriet's Ghost Still in Castle?" *Evening Telegram,* January 4, 1968.

Landfried, Ron. "Church Following Kate Smith's Wishes, Priest Says." *Lake Placid News,* June 18, 1987.

"Last Trumpet for the First Trumpeter." *Time,* July 19, 1971.

Laytner, Ron:
 "The Bizarre Saga of the World's Richest Dogs." *Tropic* (Supplement to the *Miami Herald Sun*), January 13, 1974.
 "Cool Cats, Chilly Dogs." *Chicago Tribune,* May 10, 1989.

Lednicer, Lisa Grace. "Cedar Park Is a Place People Go for Fun; Also, It's a Cemetery." *Wall Street Journal,* October 15, 1986.

Leinwand, Donna. "Waiting for His Mummy." *Miami Herald,* March 27, 1990.

Lewis, Diane. "Concerned about the Dangers Some Low-Wage and Immigrant Workers Face on the Job, Unions, Occupational Safety Groups and Some Key Members of Congress Are Wondering . . . Is It Time to Revamp OSHA?" *Boston Globe,* July 5, 1991.

Lewis, James. "Grand Mummy Clock." *Guardian,* June 15, 1972.

Liu, Cathy. "Remembering the Sticky Disaster of 1919." *Boston Globe,* January 13, 1989.

"Lucky Trousers." *American Funeral Director,* July 1988.

Lunner, Chet. "Burials in Space Get A-OK." *Florida Today,* February 13, 1985.

Luyendijk-Elshout, Antoine M. "Death Enlightened." *Journal of the American Medical Association,* April 6, 1970.

McFarland, Joseph. "Rummaging in the Museum II: The Petrified Lady." *Transactions and Studies of the College of Physicians of Philadelphia,* June 2, 1942.

McGuire, Stryker. "Death Wish Disputed." *San Antonio Light,* March 19, 1977.

"The 'Manchester Mummy' " (letter to the editor). *Middleton Guardian,* January 27, 1889.

"Man Dies Laughing at the Goodies." *Daily Mail* (London), March 29, 1975.

Marshall, Eliot. "The Hmong: Dying of Culture Shock?" *Science,* May 29, 1981.

Martin, Sylvia. "Complaint of 200-Dog-Chorus Brings Neighbors No Relief." *Sun-Sentinel,* May 10, 1967.

Mele, Chris:
 "Agreement in Works on Smith's Burial." *Adirondack Daily Enterprise,* July 22, 1987.
 "Kate Smith Will Get Her Final Wish." *Adirondack Daily Enterprise,* July 29, 1987.
 "Kate Smith's Interment Delayed." *Adirondack Daily Enterprise,* no date.
 "K. Smith's Sister Resumes Debate." *Adirondack*

Daily Enterprise, March 3, 1988.
 "Placid Bids Farewell to Kathryn: Patriot, Friend and Neighbor." *Adirondack Daily Enterprise,* November 16, 1987.
 "Smith's Interment Still on Hold." *Adirondack Daily Enterprise,* May 11, 1987.
 "Time Running Out to Bury Kate Smith This Year as Mausoleum Dispute Rages." *Adirondack Daily Enterprise,* June 24, 1987.

Melles, Ronald B., and Barrett Katz. "Sudden, Unexplained Nocturnal Death Syndrome and Night Terrors." *JAMA,* June 5, 1987.

Meyers, Dan. "A Routine Story That Got Bigger." *Philadelphia Inquirer,* January 25, 1987.

Meyers, Dan, and Frederick Cusick. "Dwyer Rejected Deal, Later Sought Pardon." *Philadelphia Inquirer,* January 24, 1987.

Michaels, Jim. "Cemetery Becomes Landmark." *San Antonio Light,* November 14, 1985.

"Milestones." *Time,* December 20, 1968.

"Milestones." *Time,* March 5, 1990.

Minor, W. F. "Solon Died 10 Years Ago." *New Orleans Times-Picayune,* August 18, 1957.

Monagan, David. "Curse of the Sleeping Death." *Science Digest,* April 1982.

Morch, Al. "Going in Style—at a Discount." *San Francisco Examiner,* April 8, 1990.

"Mortuary Has Creepy Course for Golfers." *Grand Rapids Press,* January 17, 1991.

"Mrs. F. B. Hiller's Wills." *New York Times,* May 23, 1900.

"Mrs. Frances Hiller Dead." *New York Times,* May 19, 1900.

"Mrs. Hiller's Body Laid in the Tomb." *Boston Journal,* May 21, 1900.

"Mrs. Hiller's Funeral." *New York Times,* May 27, 1900.

"Mystery Deaths in the Night." *Time,* February 23, 1981.

Neilson, Larz:
 " 'Bill Hen Two' Never Forgave Himself." *Town Crier* (Wilmington), March 9, 1983.
 "The Death of Dr. Hiller." *Town Crier* (Wilmington), September 1, 1982.
 "Dr. Henry Hiller's Medicine." *Town Crier* (Wilmington), August 18, 1982.
 "Dr. Hiller, 'The Casket Lady.' " *Town Crier* (Wilmington), July 21, 1982.
 "France's Funeral." *Town Crier* (Wilmington), March 23, 1983.
 "Henry Hiller: A Man with Three Names." *Town Crier* (Wilmington), January 26, 1983.
 "Henry Hiller's Real Estate." *Town Crier* (Wilmington), January 5, 1988.
 "How to Heft a Heavy Coffin?" *Town Crier* (Wilmington), March 2, 1983.
 " 'A Most Successful Funeral.' " *Town Crier* (Wilmington), September 8, 1982.
 "Mrs. Hiller, the Businesswoman." *Town Crier* (Wilmington), November 3, 1982.
 "Mrs. Hiller Married Her Coachman." *Town Crier* (Wilmington), December 8, 1982.
 "Mrs. Hiller Not at Her Wedding Reception." *Town Crier* (Wilmington), December 29, 1982.
 "Mrs. Hiller and the Coachman." *Town Crier* (Wilmington), December 1, 1982.
 "Mrs. Hiller Tried on Her Casket Many Times."

Town Crier (Wilmington), August 11, 1982.

"No Expenses Spared on Hiller House." *Town Crier* (Wilmington), July 28, 1982.

"Preparations for Mrs. Hiller's Burial." *Town Crier* (Wilmington), February 23, 1983.

"Reactions to the Hiller Funeral." *Town Crier* (Wilmington), April 27, 1983.

"She Grew Cranberries, He Sold Land." *Town Crier* (Wilmington), January 12, 1983.

"The Tale of the Hiller Caskets." *Town Crier* (Wilmington), August 4, 1982.

"A Torchlight Procession." *Town Crier* (Wilmington), November 10, 1982.

"The Wedding of the 'Widow of Wilmington.' " *Town Crier* (Wilmington), December 22, 1982.

"Next-to-Last Rites for Jim." *LIFE*, June 18, 1951.

Niver, Garry. "Neves Came Back from the Dead." *Times* (San Mateo, Calif.), April 30, 1990.

Nolan, Bruce. "Thousands Attend Memorial Services Given for Satchmo." *Times-Picayune*, July 12, 1971.

"Noted Lawyer Laid to Rest." *Semi-Weekly Sentinel* (Le Mars, Iowa), September 16, 1930.

"Noted Lawyer Passes Away." *Semi-Weekly Sentinel* (Le Mars, Iowa), September 12, 1930.

Oppenheimer, Robert. "Einstein's Science, Einstein's Faith; an Appreciation by Dr. Oppenheimer." *Princeton Packet*, April 28, 1955.

"Orioles Grant Fan's Last Wish." *American Funeral Director*, January 1989.

"Our Towns." *Chicago Tribune*, January 13, 1991.

"Paints Hazeltine as Giver." *Los Angeles Times*, February 12, 1926.

"Panzran to His Death on Gibbet." *Leavenworth Times*, September 5, 1930.

"Par for the Corpse." *Sports Illustrated*, February 4, 1991.

Park, Edwards. "Without Warning, Molasses in January Surged over Boston." *Smithsonian*, November 1983.

"Petticoat Acts as Will." *Los Angeles Times*, July 1, 1925.

"Petticoat Will Case Appraisal Filed with Court." *Los Angeles Times*, October 8, 1925.

"Petticoat Will Fight On." *Los Angeles Times*, February 2, 1926.

"Petticoat Will Given Support." *Los Angeles Times*, February 11, 1926.

" 'Petticoat' Will Held to Be Valid." *Los Angeles Times*, April 1, 1927.

"Petticoat Will Motion to Be Heard March 4." *Los Angeles Times*, February 20, 1926.

"Philanthropy: Going to the Dogs." *Newsweek*, February 4, 1974.

"Police Say Chaplin Grave Robbers Caught after Watch on 200 Telephones Kiosks." *Times*, May 18, 1978.

Powell, Larry. "Casey Jones: Always on Time." *Mississippi*, March-April 1986.

"Public Now Barred at Valentino's Bier." *New York Times*, August 26, 1926.

Queenan, Joe. "Skeleton Keys." *Wall Street Journal*, February 12, 1991.

"Ralph Neves: Pronounced Dead after Bay Meadows Spill, Jockey Revives." *San Francisco Chronicle*, May 9, 1936.

Ranalli, Ralph. "Dorchester Laundry Worker Killed after Falling in Dryer." *Boston Herald*, November 22, 1990.

"Recluse's Hoard Claimed." *Los Angeles Times*, February 1, 1926.

Redford, Sara L. "Hundreds See Reuben Smith's Burial." *Amesbury News Souvenir*, August 14, 1968.

Reeves, Scott, and Jim Steinberg. "Marijuana Found in Burrus' System." *Fresno Bee*, November 3, 1990.

Rich, Donna Bozza. "A Funeral Home for Those on the Go." *Virginian-Pilot*, April 16, 1991.

Roberts, John. "Peerless Satchmo Silenced by Death." *Times-Picayune*, July 7, 1971.

Robinson, Monroe Douglas. "Henderson House." *Harper's Bazaar*, July 1939.

"Roebuck May Argue Millar Mother Race Defies Public Good." *Toronto Daily Star*, November 6, 1936.

"Sandra West's Death Ruled an Accidental Overdose." *San Antonio Light*, July 19, 1977.

"Scenes of Anguish at Relief Station." *Boston Daily Globe*, January 16, 1919.

Schoettler, Carl. "A Reverent Resting Place for Dear Departed Pets." *Evening Sun*, October 5, 1965.

Schonberg, Harold C. "Big Voice, Big Temperament." *New York Times*, October 25, 1959.

Seaver, Lynda. "Going in Style." *Tribune*, October 1, 1990.

Seligmann, Jean, Joe Contreras, and Peter Rinearson. "The Curse of the Hmong." *Newsweek*, August 10, 1981.

"Settlement in Petticoat Will." *Los Angeles Times*, April 3, 1927.

"Silent Crowds See Valentino's Cortege; Screen Stars Weep." *New York Times*, August 31, 1926.

"Sits in Sarcophagus." *Boston Globe*, January 26, 1899.

"Skirt-Will Suit Lost by Nurses." *Los Angeles Times*, March 11, 1931.

Smith, Geoffrey. "A Farewell to Malcolm." *Financial World*, March 6, 1990.

Smith, Herbert W. "The Manchester Mummy." *Manchester Faces and Places*, April 1903.

Smith, Tamera. "How Much Longer? Gary Wrote to Nicole." *Deseret News*, January 17, 1977.

Smolowe, Jill. "A Frenzied Farewell." *Time*, June 19, 1989.

Snow, Deborah. "Cemetery's Part Zoo, Museum and Arboretum." *Southtown Economist*, February 14, 1991.

Solomon, David J. "Sometimes It Seems People Are a Bit Obsessed with Convenience." *Wall Street Journal*, June 15, 1987.

Sorensen, George A. "Execution: Frantic to End." *Salt Lake Tribune*, January 18, 1977.

"Soviet Forest Lawn." *Parade*, August 18, 1974.

Starzl, Rita. " 'Womanless Library' Was One Man's Dream." *Semi-Weekly Sentinel* (Le Mars, Iowa), March 28, 1991.

Steinberg, Jim, and Scott Reeves. "Death Took Center Stage." *Fresno Bee*, November 2, 1990.

Steinburg, Lynn. " 'Till Death Do Us Part." *Los Angeles Times*, August 13, 1989.

Stevens, William K. "Official Calls in Press and Kills Himself." *New York Times*, January 23, 1987.

"Struggle in Sticky Fluid." *Boston Post*, January 15, 1919.

"Successor to Bilbo, Dead of Long Illness, Unlikely Until Fall." *Washington Star*, August 22, 1947.

Sudetic, Chuck. "For Well-Housed Dead, TV and Other Comforts." *New York Times*, February 19, 1991.

Sullivan, Barbara. "It's Like Disneyland; It's Like a Zoo—It's a Cemetery." *Chicago Tribune*, August 11, 1983.

"The Talk of the Town." *New Yorker*, July 17, 1971.

Taubman, Howard. "Leonard Warren Collapses and Dies on Stage at 'Met.' " *New York Times*, March 5, 1960.

"Third 'Petticoat Will' Suit." *Los Angeles Times*, July 31, 1925.

Thomas, Jack. "71 Years after the Flood, He's Still a Survivor." *Boston Globe*, January 15, 1990.

"Thousands in Riot at Valentino Bier; More than 100 Hurt." *New York Times*, August 25, 1926.

"Thousands of Pets Are Buried at Bonheur Memorial Park and Each Has a Story." *Evening Sun*, June 22, 1960.

"Tracking Down the Real Casey Jones." *Southern Living*, May 1981.

Trombla, Ted. "Reuben Smith's Curious Wish." *Yankee*, November 1963.

Tyner, Howard A. "Moscow Cemetery a Living Shrine." *Chicago Tribune*, May 21, 1984.

"Undertaker Will Offer New Drive-in Service." *New York Times*, March 14, 1968.

"The Unread Part of the Statement." *Philadelphia Inquirer*, January 25, 1987.

Valdivia, Angela, and Ellen Clear. "Burial Stunt Kills Fresnan." *Fresno Bee*, November 11, 1990.

Van Atta, Dale. "Prisoner 13871 Was Never Candidate for Sainthood, As Crime Record Attests." *Deseret News*, January 17, 1977.

"Warren Famed for Verdi Roles." *New York Times*, March 5, 1960.

"Wealthy Canines Lead a Dog's Life." *Valley News Dispatch* (New Kensington, Pa.), September 7, 1972.

Weaver, Michael S. "Père Lachaise: The Dead 'Live.' " *Chicago Tribune*, October 26, 1986.

Wentworth, Philip. "Notes and Sketches by the Way: Middleton to Manchester." *Middleton Guardian*, October 24, 1885.

West, Fran. "70 years Ago a Legend Was Born in Yazoo Amid Splinters of the Famed Cannonball." *Yazoo City Herald*, April 30, 1970.

"When Politics Was a Family Business." *U.S. News & World Report*, November 14, 1988.

"Will Signature Attacked." *Los Angeles Times*, February 3, 1926.

"With His Talking Tombstone, John Dilks Gives Everyone a Chance to Have the Last Word." *People*, November 7, 1977.

"Wobbly." *New Yorker*, December 19, 1988.

"Wonder in Life, Mystery in Death." *Boston Globe*, May 19, 1900.

Yap, E. H., et al. "*Pseudomonas Pseudomallei* and Sudden Unexplained Death in Thai Construction Workers." *Lancet*, August 11, 1990.

"Yardbird Keith Relf Dead at 33." *Rolling Stone*, June 17, 1976.

Yardley, Jim:

"Animal Lovers Rally to Save Goat's Life." *Atlanta Journal-Constitution*, May 21, 1991.

"Goat Finds Refuge in Noah's Ark." *Atlanta Journal-Constitution*, May 22, 1991.

"Goat Kills Cherokee Man Who Taught Him to Be

'Mean.'" *Atlanta Journal-Constitution,* May 17, 1991.

"Goat May Be Allowed to Live at Sanctuary." *Atlanta Journal-Constitution,* May 21, 1991.

"Killer Goat's Fate Undecided." *Atlanta Journal-Constitution,* May 20, 1991.

"Snowball's Chance Improves." *Atlanta Journal-Constitution,* May 23, 1991.

"Zink Will is Limelight." *Semi-Weekly Sentinel* (Le Mars, Iowa), September 23, 1930.

Other

"All Things Considered." Radio transcript. Washington, D.C.: NPR, August 16, 1991.

American Society for the Prevention of Cruelty to Animals. File note re: P. T. Barnum, no date. American Society for the Prevention of Cruelty to Animals, New York.

"Annual Report of Park Commissioners." *Municipal Register* (Bridgeport, Conn.), April 1898.

Barnum, P. T. Letter to Henry Bergh. March 11, 1867. American Society for the Prevention of Cruelty to Animals, New York.

Barnum, P. T. Will of Phineas Taylor Barnum. March 30, 1891.

Bell, Mrs. Alexander Graham. Letter written to Mrs. Gilbert Grosvenor. August 2, 1922. Bell Family Papers. Baddeck, Nova Scotia: Alexander Graham Bell National Historic Site.

Bergh, Henry. Letter to Archibald Russell. January 7, 1867. American Society for the Prevention of Cruelty to Animals, New York.

Bergh, Henry. Letter to P. T. Barnum. December 11, 1866. American Society for the Prevention of Cruelty to Animals, New York.

Bergh, Henry. Letter to P. T. Barnum. March 7, 1867. American Society for the Prevention of Cruelty to Animals, New York.

Bergh, Henry. Letter to P. T. Barnum. April 13, 1880. American Society for the Prevention of Cruelty to Animals, New York.

Bergh, Henry. Letter to P. T. Barnum. August 17, 1885. American Society for the Prevention of Cruelty to Animals, New York.

Boarss, Edwin C. "Law Enforcement at Fort Smith, 1871-1896." Unpublished manuscript. Arkansas: National Park Service, 1962.

"Carolyn Matsumoto." Police report. Berkeley, Calif.: Berkeley Police Department, May 16, 1984.

Cashman, George L. "The Fantastic Episode at Lincoln's Tomb." News release. Springfield, Ill.: Ridge Cemetery, 1960.

"Castro, Alfredo—Sudden Death." Police report. Boston: Boston Police Department, November 21, 1990.

"Collision of Trains 1 and 83." Interoffice report. Chicago: Central Railroad, May 10, 1900.

Court documents and affidavits pertaining to Cecil George Harris, deceased, dated June 15, 16, and 22, 1948; filed in the Surrogate Court of the Judicial District of Kerrobert, Saskatchewan, Canada.

"Description of Prisoner—Jefferson Baldwin," Salem: Oregon State, June 24, 1915.

Dinsmoor, S. P. "Pictorial History of the Cabin Home in Garden of Eden." Guidebook. Lucas, Kans.: no date.

Fairchild, Mrs. David. Letter written to Mr. and Mrs. Gilbert Grosvenor. August 6, 1922. Baddeck, Nova Scotia: Alexander Graham Bell National Historic Park.

"Fatal Ice Cream Accident." Press release. Tampa: Tampa Police Department, April 9, 1991.

"Flyers to Establish Memorial to Kate Smith." Philadelphia Flyers news release. Philadelphia: June 4, 1987.

"Forest Lawn Memorial-Park, Glendale." Pictorial map and guide. Glendale, Calif.: Forest Lawn, no date.

"Free Burial Service for Organ Donor." News release. Chicago: Cedar Park Cemetery and Cedar Park Funeral Home, June 20, 1984.

"Free Funeral & Burial for Victims of Drunken Driving Accidents." News release. Chicago: Cedar Park Cemetery and Cedar Park Funeral Home, May 5, 1987.

"Free Grave for Victims of Drug Abuse." News release. Chicago: Cedar Park Cemetery and Cedar Park Funeral Home, September 19, 1986.

"Free Grave for Victims of Hand Guns." News release. Chicago: Cedar Park Cemetery and Cedar Park Funeral Home, May 20, 1985.

"Garden of Eden." Information pamphlet. Lucas, Kans.: Garden of Eden, no date.

Haskett, Delmas D., and William M. Reaves. "Oakdale Cemetery Records, Wilmington, North Carolina (1852-1879)." Wilmington, N.C.: New Hanover County Public Library, 1989.

" 'Heaven Can Wait' 10K (6.2 Mile) Run." News release. Chicago: Cedar Park Cemetery and Cedar Park Funeral Home, May 4, 1987.

"H.L.A. Services Inc." U.S. Department of Labor's Occupational Safety and Health Administration. OSHA list of H.L.A.'s violations. Boston: OSHA, March 1, 1991.

Isay, David. "Morning Edition." Radio transcript on Dick Falk. Washington, D.C.: NPR, July 10, 1991.

"Kate and the Flyers." Philadelphia Flyers news release. Philadelphia: Spectrum, no date.

"Kate Smith Statue." Philadelphia Flyers news release. Philadelphia: Spectrum, no date.

"Leonard Warren: Biography." Press release. New York: Hurok Attractions, no date.

Letter confirming date of incarceration and execution of Gary Gilmore. Records office. Draper, Utah: Utah State Prison, October 23, 1991.

Mascai, Gwen. "All Things Considered." Radio transcript on Ahlgrim's Funeral Home. Washington, D.C.: NPR, June 24, 1991.

"Museum Panel to Set Scientific and Historic Precedents with Recommendation on Proposal to Clone Lincoln's DNA; Many Questions Remain." News release. Washington, D.C.: National Museum of Health & Medicine Foundation, April 26, 1991.

Nash, Thomas. Last codicil of the will of Colonel Thomas Nash. Proved 1813.

Official death row logbook entries. Record of prisoners admittance and death dates. San Quentin State Prison, no date.

Over, William H. "Life of Sitting Bull." Brochure. Vermillion, S. Dak.: University of South Dakota, 1950.

Record of prisoner Carl Panzran and execution date. Leavenworth, Kans.: United States Penitentiary, no date.

Ritchie, Eleanor E. Last will and testament of Eleanor E. Ritchie and first codicil. Dated March 20, 1963 and April 12, 1963.

"The Scott-Ritchey Program." Pamphlet. Auburn, Ala.: College of Veterinary Medicine, Auburn University, 1985.

Secretary of state vital records returns. *Death Register.* Boston: Commonwealth of Massachusetts, 1872.

Shannon, Margaret. "The Ritchey Bequest: Millions for Small Animal Research." Auburn, Ala.: Auburn University, no date.

Stanley, Leo L. "He Blew His Top." Unpublished manuscript kept at San Quentin State Prison. San Quentin, Calif.: no date.

"Thomas Jefferson's Last Words." Office report. Charlottesville, Va.: Monticello, June 7, 1988.

"Throttle in His Hand." Bio by unknown author on file at Ricks Memorial Library. Yazoo City, Miss.: July 9, 1948.

"Tribute Programs." Information pamphlet for customers. Spokane, Wash.: National Music Service, 1989.

"Tribute Programs." Information pamphlet for funeral directors. Spokane, Wash.: National Music Service, 1989.

INDEX

**Library of Congress
Cataloging-in-Publication Data**
Shadows of death / by the editors of Time-Life
Books.
p.   cm.   (Library of curious and unusual facts).
Includes bibliographical references and index.
ISBN 0-8094-7719-X
ISBN 0-8094-7720-3 (lib. bdg.)
1. Death—Social aspects—Miscellanea.
2. Curiosities and wonders.
I. Time-Life Books. II. Series.
HQ1073.S48 1992
306.9—dc20   91-36346 CIP

LIBRARY OF CURIOUS AND UNUSUAL FACTS

This volume is one in a series that explores
astounding but surprisingly true events in history,
science, nature, and human conduct. Other books in
the series include:

*For information on and a full description of any of
the Time-Life Books series listed above, please call
1-800-621-7026 or write:*
Reader Information
Time-Life Customer Service
P.O. Box C-32068
Richmond, Virginia 23261-2068